REMEMBERING WHO WE ARE

LAARKMAA'S GUIDANCE ON HEALING THE HUMAN CONDITION

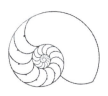

PIA SMITH ORLEANE, PH.D.
&
CULLEN BAIRD SMITH

BALBOA.
PRESS

A DIVISION OF HAY HOUSE

Remembering Who We Are
Laarkmaa's Guidance on Healing the Human Condition

Cover Design and Book Layout by Chris Molé

Includes Original Art by Ann DiSalvo

Author Photos by Judith Pavlik

Balboa Press books may be ordered through booksellers or by contacting:

Balboa Press
A Division of Hay House
1663 Liberty Drive
Bloomington, IN 47403
www.balboapress.com
1-(877) 407-4847

ISBN: 978-1-4525-7226-0 (sc)
ISBN: 978-1-4525-7227-7 (hc)
ISBN: 978-1-4525-7228-4 (e)

Library of Congress Control Number: 2013907182

Printed in the United States of America.

Balboa Press rev. date: 06/04/2013

Dedicated to all who have enough love
and courage to make the necessary changes
for human evolution.

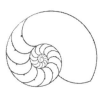

CONTENTS

FOREWORD

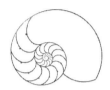

This unusual and important book is a creative manifestation stemming from a remarkable collaboration: between a collective of loving and beneficent, interstellar beings known as Laarkmaa, and two humans—a devoted couple, Pia Smith Orleane and Cullen Baird Smith—who are emissaries of Laarkmaa's wise counsel and the profoundly loving energy frequencies that they bring to share with us here on Earth. Through Pia and Cullen, this book is a bridge between the Pleiadians, who have achieved living in oneness as an entire society, and our human race, our global collective in which we all experience the crippling effects of separation—the belief that we are separate from one another and from our original divine Source. This belief in separation, and the energetic consequences of our behaviors that result from our belief, leaves us feeling stuck and powerless, suffering through all manner of fear and doubt, anger and judgment, victim-consciousness, disease, and the experience of lack.

Laarkmaa has brought forth this book to assist us to heal every one of these conditions, and to show us how we may create for ourselves, individually and collectively, an ongoing and sustained state of loving embrace, compassion, trust, joy, and peace. Their only "agenda" is to help us open to more love, so that we may heal ourselves and the planet, fully transcending all suffering and fear, and join them in oneness. This is nothing less than healing the human condition. From the most dedicated lightworkers—or as Laarkmaa says, "light movers"—to those just awakening on their spiritual pathways, and for all who are interested in opening their hearts to greater love and healing, this deeply valuable guidance will be welcome, indeed.

Laarkmaa says this book is about health—yet with that one word, they encompass a cornucopia of meaning and opportunity. The health they envision for us involves all aspects of our beings—physical, mental, emotional, and spiritual; healing the whole of ourselves, as we remember more and more of Who We Are.

Laarkmaa emphasizes the energetic foundation of all things, and because, they tell us, *everything* is energy, they encourage us to greater awareness of the nature of energy in our own bodies and beings. Beyond the common understanding of spiritual healing, for instance, they teach us that much of what we ingest does damage to our spiritual beings—not only harmful food and drink, but also the disharmonious energies we take into our beings through competitive cultural practices, our fear-based nightly news, violent movies, and much more. We are harmed as well by the toxic energies of our own unrestrained and unconscious negative thinking. These disruptive, unaligned energies actually rip and tear our etheric bodies, causing damage to our etheric blueprints, which is then translated into physical disease and aging for us personally.

In addition, because we are a part of All That Is, Laarkmaa tells us that everything we think, feel, say, do, and experience within ourselves affects everyone, everywhere. In order, then, to heal ourselves and the planet, and to participate responsibly in our interstellar relationships, we must change our behaviors;

in order to change our behaviors, we must understand the emotional issues that underlie our choices.

This book is deeply about choice. In clear and simple language yet with profound wisdom, Laarkmaa shows us how every moment of our daily life is ripe with opportunities to break free of our behavioral patterns and to choose to create the change required for us to transcend our current levels of limitation. Laarkmaa asks us to engage our hearts fully in our lives, in every choice. They ask us to stretch ourselves, embracing responsibility for change, both in our individual lives and for the evolution of humanity, and also expanding into conscious participation with the evolution of Earth Herself.

A vastly important area of choice and change for each of us relates to our emotional patterning and habitual reactions. Laarkmaa offers rich new insight on behavioral patterns, through detailed descriptions of how our individual habits of self-judgment and emotional reaction, and our ingrained collective, cultural beliefs, become so established within us. Working deeply to uncover and resolve our hidden, subconscious beliefs that fuel our emotional reactions is essential to healing. Laarkmaa calls this *shadow work*, and invites us to courageous emotional honesty so that we may learn to create consciously rather than by default, through unconscious thoughts and behaviors.

From their loving Pleiadian perspective, Laarkmaa provides us a comprehensive overview of the aspects of living in the third dimension, with new understandings of the challenges of duality, including the split between the heart and the mind. They show us how to unify and create harmony from opposite polarities, so that, at the deepest levels, we may move beyond our current focus on differences, toward honoring what we share in oneness. In this way, we learn to transform our beliefs from the old paradigms and to release judgment, which are crucial choices for spiritual evolution as well as for healing on all levels within ourselves. Expanding their commentary on our experience in third dimension, Laarkmaa also discusses the mental aspects of time and dimension; the physical aspects of being, including our sexuality; the physical-etheric relationship; and moving light.

One of the beauties of this book is that Laarkmaa shares with us not dry, theoretical concepts, but dynamic, living wisdom and practical approaches to change that enhance our ability to live our lives in beauty, grace, love, truth, and joy. They give us "tools for change," practical and effective ways to *apply* deeper understanding in our lives. These useful tools and understandings are expressed simply and in multiple repetitions that assist us to grasp the meaning of what Laarkmaa wishes to convey.

Laarkmaa guides us in how to restore our own emotional balance, in part through their exciting interpretations and exercises using the frequencies and healing qualities of colors and numbers. Throughout the book, they offer new information from various points of view, not only broadening our perspective of the energetic and symbolic significance of colors and numbers individually, but also showing us how to use colors and number frequencies together, merging and blending the energies to enhance our healing process.

Laarkmaa teaches us how to work with pain and how to increase our will power; they address our life purpose, and share with us a wonderful Heart Meditation. Having helped us understand how we have become so unbalanced and diseased, they teach us to use the Elements of Foundation, the Seven Components of Healing, and a Rainbow of Healing Essences, so that we may transform ourselves into the whole and healthy beings we are meant to be.

With penetrating insight, Laarkmaa offers new thinking to expand our concepts of community and living in transparency, and to illustrate the influence of technology and competition in our individual lives and in our collective experience of reality. Laarkmaa asks us to widen our limited perspective of androgyny, showing us the importance of fully integrating within ourselves the Divine Feminine and Divine Masculine energies and attributes that are a natural part of who we are.

At Laarkmaa's request, Pia and Cullen have written the tenth chapter. From a Pleiadian-human perspective, these two dedicated and loving "light movers" have created a novel and insightful interpretation of two sets of religious guidelines for living: the Christian tradition's Ten Commandments and the Buddhist tradition's Noble Eightfold Path to Wisdom. Expanding beyond that, in a potent summation bringing together the power of intention and the activation of will in service to love and oneness, Pia and Cullen have created a Pleiadian-inspired set of guidelines for conscious living, The Ten Choices, as a reminder of the significance of our own choices in creating the change we wish to see in our lives and on our planet. These are inspiring choices for responsible living in spiritual maturity, contributing consciously to the well-being of the whole of life.

If it brings your heart joy to imagine a world of cooperation, harmony, and peace, with love, trust, compassion, and joy as constant companions in your feeling states; if it excites you to imagine *knowing* yourself to be absolutely free and utterly safe, then this book will touch your heart and inspire you to the transformations that each of us must actively choose in order to bring forth this magnificent new reality.

As we sow the seeds of conscious choice for change, we are together creating a harvest of resurrection and joy for all to share. As we approach the whole of our lives as sacred, loving and nurturing ourselves and all things in creation as a part of divine Source; as we do our inner work to resolve our shadows and reclaim our inherent perfection as a part of Source; as we honor ourselves as powerful creators and take responsibility for what we choose to create, we are then resurrecting ourselves, guided by our own heart's truth and creating our Rainbow bodies of complete unification, wholeness and ascension.

With integrity, grace and generosity of heart, and with enormous love for all of us, Laarkmaa gives us the keys to our own freedom and shares guidance for aligning with universal truth. It is time to step into planetary and even galactic responsibility—and it all begins within each one of us, in every choice we make. Then together, in powerful amplification of what we are creating individually, we may weave threads of conscious intention and loving choice to create a beautiful tapestry of manifested reality, focused through love, that will carry us into the new Earth, as we remember Who We Are; as we heal ourselves and the whole of humanity; and as we finally return in conscious awareness to the our divine origins, in love and oneness with All That Is.

> AMARA ELIANE, Author,
> *The Wisdom of the Heart: Love-Centered Guidance for Spiritual Mastery from the Ancients, Ascended Masters, and the Realms of Light* (in press).
> Mount Shasta, California

PREFACE

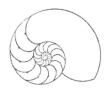

For several years now, people who are interested in human evolution have been asking for Laarkmaa's next book. Who is Laarkmaa? They are a loving group of Pleiadians, dedicated to guiding humanity, who describe themselves as "one of six and six of one." Our ability to think of them as a constellation of individual personalities unified within one group can help us to understand how we ourselves are moving away from individuality and into a shared unity. In our first book, *Conversations With Laarkmaa, A Pleiadian View of the New Reality,* we told the story of how and why Laarkmaa came to us.

We may be evolving as a species, yet we still have many places where we are blind to our habitual belief systems and patterns of behavior. In fact, these belief systems and habitual patterns are so ingrained that we sometimes cannot find our way out of them. Laarkmaa tells us that if we want to evolve to our fullest potential, if we wish to be healthy, and if we want to experience lives of joy and abundance, we must simply remember Who We Are. Once we remember, everything is possible.

You will probably not discover anything in this book that is completely new. In fact, you may find yourself saying, "I knew that!" We hope that what you find here will feel very familiar and ring true to you. Laarkmaa says that all wisdom is already in our hearts, so every aspect of the truth they share here can be verified through the resonance you feel in your own hearts. The point of this book, according to Laarkmaa, is to help us to *remember* in order for us to heal ourselves from the illusions that keep us sick, scared, and separate.

The concepts Laarkmaa presents require few words to explain. Yet they have given us a plethora of words, weaving concepts together from various positions and perspectives in order to be *sure* we understand. You will find certain themes reappearing over and over again in various chapters. Laarkmaa repeats their wisdom in multiple ways in order for us to integrate their information and to implement the changes we need to make. The concepts will spiral around and around, raising our awareness to new levels and opening us to the possibilities for healing ourselves and our planet. Laarkmaa's words help us to see beyond our limited perspectives.

These messages have been given to humanity by interstellar beings who do not speak as we do. They communicate through tones, heart to heart, merging with us (Cullen and Pia) to place their messages first into our hearts, and then using what they call "the libraries of our brains" to find words that match their message and express the heart-wisdom they are here to share. They communicate in a way that brings their information to us around and around in spirals that are often repetitive; through the repetitions they remind us that our evolution is also a spiral- ing process. Each word is imbued with the energy of Laarkmaa's love. As we have edited this work, we have done our best to keep the purity of the message, yet to transform it into a linear flow that we hope is easy to follow. Because Laarkmaa speaks in spirals, and we humans read in a linear fashion, this has been an arduous process. It has been our heartfelt intention to present these valuable messages in a flow that is clear and easily readable, so that everyone may benefit. We ask you to bear with the repetitions in the book, because Laarkmaa feels they are important.

This book is lovingly offered by our Pleiadian friends to help us remember Who We Are. We no longer need to suffer under the illusions that have caused us fear and separation. We no longer need to judge or compete with one another. When we drop the belief systems that support old paradigms, we open the way to create a world of beauty, love, trust, joy, compassion, and abundance. Contained within these pages are new ways of thinking, but more importantly, you will find guidelines here on how, through our hearts, we can *feel* our way towards the truth of Who We Are and who we always have been. We are here in human form with one purpose: to love each other and the world. Laarkmaa tells us that we can distill that purpose into two words that will guide us: BE LOVE.

With these two words in our hearts, we present to you Laarkmaa's guidance on healing the human condition.

Pia Orleane

LAARKMAA'S INTRODUCTION:
REMEMBERING

The focus of this book is to help humans understand how you may evolve into a state of continual health. By focusing on health, you focus on the evolution of humanity through reclaiming your own divinity: you are beings of love. You carry light and love within you, yet you have forgotten that. We share these words with you in order to help you remember Who You Are.

You have within you the strongest force in the universe, the power of love. Yet so often, you allow another force (fear) to govern your thoughts, your actions, and the beliefs you build through your experiences. Within these pages, we will convey to you a pathway that supports your stepping outside of your fears and healing all of your dis-ease. We will show you how to love your shadows until they are dissolved. As you learn the many aspects and elements of love and light that we will share, you will begin to understand that you have a choice, and that you can create healthier, more abundant lives by making that choice.

Currently, humans have a very third-dimensional way of looking at health; you compartmentalize symptoms and pathologized problems rather than looking at the root cause of dis-ease. We have a more universal view, and in our view, health is much simpler than that. Health comes from love. In fact, health *is* love. Dis-ease comes from fear. In fact, disease *is* fear. You have not had health explained to you in this fashion before. The only thing necessary for you to heal is for you to remember Who You Are, for when you remember Who You Are, you can heal all that you are not. You have forgotten that you are divine parts of Source and that you have the power to co-create total health. To heal, you must remember Who You Are: beings who come from divine love.

There are only two forces in the universe: love and fear. You know this; you have just forgotten. Humans are not aware that all of the complications that make up your lives can be pared down to only these two forces: love and fear. *Everything* you think, feel, and do comes from and is connected to one of these two elements. One of these forces (love) promotes your health, your abundance, and your total well-being. The other force (fear) causes you dis-ease. One of these forces (fear) traps you in third-dimensional pain and separation. The other force (love) dissolves all fear and frees you to remember your true essence. All of the fears and manifestations of fear that are character-ized as anger, grief, greed, jealousy, judgment, frustration, war, etc., are locked within the cells of your body and have kept you in dis-eased states because of the separation these fears have created. We, Laarkmaa, differentiate between emotions (which all stem from fear) and your natural higher vibratory feeling states, which are love, trust, joy, and compassion.

When humans live in love rather than in fear, your bodies do not have to deal with toxic overloads or traumas and issues that have arisen out of karmic choices made through fear, the erroneous choices you made in blind efforts to keep yourselves safe. We are here to share with you that safety and health exist within your own hearts. It is when you allow the presence of fear and all that fear can manifest through your emotions that dis-ease begins.

If you are thinking or acting through unconditional love without any agenda, you are using the greatest force in the universe: true love. If you are thinking or acting with concern, worry, grief, frustration, anger, disappointment, or any of the myriad emotions that often shape the course and direction of human lives, you are acting out of fear. Fear is the ultimate cause of all discomfort within the human species. You get stuck in your belief systems and confused about what makes you feel safe or what makes you feel "OK." The only things required for any human to be OK are to accept the truth that you are loveable and to give love continually to everyone you meet and every situation that comes to you. This energy is then reflected back to you, reinforcing the fact that you are loveable. You are designed so that the divine light within each of you may reflect back and forth to one another continually; the constant reflection of love is the true state of ultimate health.

Another word for fear is dis-ease, for fear is nothing other than being "out of ease" with Who You Are. Through fear (or dis-ease), you step away from your divinity, not understanding the divine power that each human carries as part of Source. Each of you is a co-creator, yet humanity at this time sleeps, unaware of your co-creative abilities. You have forgotten your power, and you allow yourselves to be ruled by the many fears that masquerade as misunderstandings and false beliefs. The only true fear, which is the root of all emotions, is the fear of not being loved or not being able to love. That fear comes from the sleep of forgetfulness. You have forgotten that not only can you love and be loved, you *are* love. Dear Ones, the future humans that you are re-remembering yourselves into being *are love*. When you experience yourselves as love, and you live your lives through that experience, you are in harmony. You are then operating under the universal principle of the highest power in the universe: love. If you are *not* operating from that principle, then you are operating out of fear. Acting from fear causes you to move into states of dis-ease. Your physical, mental, and emotional systems alert you that something is out of balance by showing you continual dis-ease. We tell you again, what you call disease (dis-ease) is nothing more than being out of harmony.

Humans need to learn how to dwell consistently in the frequency of love so that you do not misuse your valuable energy or jeopardize your vibratory connections with your etheric selves through vibrating at lower, denser levels that are full of fear. You need to practice moving past any type of fear, directly into the energy of love. A continual return to the state of love provides a higher vibration that allows your etheric bodies to reflect wholeness to your physical bodies, thereby supporting complete health. We will discuss more about this throughout this book.

The purpose of this book is to give you a broader perspective of the aspects and elements of fear and love and to help you remember Who You Are. The concepts are simple, so they do not require very many words to explain, but we will repeat them throughout the book many times for your integration. Putting the concepts into practice is *your* work, and we trust that you will find joy in doing so. We will speak about the Split of Duality that has caused you to allow fear into your lives, and how that split causes conflict. We will explain to you how the third-dimensional mental, emotional, and physical aspects keep you constricted, and we will talk about your life's purpose. We will share with you a rainbow of healing essences, give you a description of the seven components of healing, and help you to create a new foundation for Who You Are becoming. We will tell you how to bring harmony to your world and create more functional and peaceful communities. We have even ordered the chapters to correspond with the energy that mathematically matches what we present. We will include answers to some of your most frequently asked questions in what we share, for so many of you struggle with the same issues. We trust that our perspective will help you move beyond your challenges into a more joyful and connective existence. As we speak to you throughout this book, we will show you how to begin your healing. Healing the human condition is about simply forgetting all that you have believed and remembering the truth of Who You Are. We wish to help you to remember *all* that you have forgotten. We love you, and we are here to help.

With love and light,
LAARKMAA

Chapter One

ENERGY

*"The first thing to remember to
begin healing is that everything
is energy."*

Everything is Energy

The first step to remembering is to understand what unity is. The illusions of duality have caused you to forget the principles of unity and to believe that you are separate. In unity, everything is connected. This means that even the two forces, love and fear, are connected in unity. How you relate to these forces and work with them depends upon your perceptions and misperceptions about the power they carry. To comprehend the powers of each, you must understand that both love and fear are forms of energy.

Everything is energy. *Everything.* You need to understand how energy manifests into form and how to work with all energy in order to be actively involved in co-creation. In your third-dimensional reality, your physical form is the densest manifestation of all energy. Energy goes through a specific process, which you desperately need to understand, in order to come into a physical form. This process begins with energy as intention. Humanity is confused about how intentions are manifested into physical form. You believe that intentions originate in the mind and are then sent into the universe to come into form. Actually, to manifest into form, an intention needs to be directed by your will, channeled through your heart, and then sent to the brain for activation and distribution. Intentions come from the connection between the light of Source and your light, where they meet at your will center (in your physical solar plexus area). As you use your will to focus your intentions, you are able to send the energy of manifestation upwards into your hearts, where you can experience further connection.

Currently in most humans, a block exists between your will centers and your hearts, so intentions bypass the heart and go directly to the mind, where your thought energy often becomes chaotic, without the guidance of will. The mind alone is not a vehicle for creation. Thoughts that originate without the heart's guidance are disconnected from Source. When this happens, which is the way most of humanity thinks, the energy of thought is utilized in confused and disconnected ways, manifesting through mental thoughts that are fueled by the emotions, beliefs, and attachments to past and future experiences. This chaotic presentation of thought energy, fired freely without any guidance, direction, or regulation from your will center (your source of light), or any connection to the wisdom of love in your hearts, causes you to co-create a chaotic physicality. Collectively, humanity has agreed to this manner of manifestation, which is why you have such similar and strong beliefs about what is "real." You have agreed to create it in this way, and you have forgotten that chaotic thoughts powered by misunderstood emotions create a random and chaotic world. You need a clearer understanding of energy and how energy manifests through the application of will and the proper channeling of intentions.

Your physical forms, of course, reflect the sequential actions of how you channel your thoughts. Both what you take in from the collective energies around you and what you generate from the energy of your own thoughts and emotions contributes to the creation of your physical forms, individually and collectively. Creation of health moves from energy in the form of intention, channeled through the will, to the heart, to the mind, and then into physical form. Creation of dis-ease occurs when you move energy in a chaotic and disconnected pattern through your minds without the participation of your hearts or will. Emotions alert you to the fact that you are suffering under illusions of separation and misalignment from the universal energy of unity. Many of you are now experiencing a re-connective process where you are realigning your hearts and minds through the use of your will, disconnecting old patterns in order to step away from the illusions of dis-ease and return to a state of ultimate health. We wish to help you in this process.

Your physical forms are going through purification as you experience places of disharmony in order to return to a state of balance and connection to Source. The secret for success in purification, as we will explain later, is to release all judgments about the process and continually turn your thoughts to love. Focused, will-directed, heart-guided, intentional thoughts of trust and gratitude will help you to manifest a world filled with love and light rather than a world filled with fear, competition, and conflict. As all of you begin to do this together, you will move more quickly into the experience of harmonious unity for the highest good of all. Remember: you—and everything else—are energy. And *all* energy is connected.

The Energy of Instinct

You arrived on this planet with full knowledge and remembrance of Who You Are as energetic beings. You remembered everything that comprises the seven components of healing, and you remembered how to use the rainbow essences that we will describe later. You remembered them because they are part of you; you remembered them as you brought them into form in third-dimensional physicality. You also arrived with an instinct that was part of who you were then and will always be a part of you. It is the part that you have subsequently forgotten; it is the part that can remind you to continually come back to the energy of love in any given moment, for that is the true basis of your being. Your true basis of being will *always* be love. However, your environment soon caused you to begin to forget this.

In duality, you forgot that you had the power to choose love, and through choices based on fear, you began to make greater and greater separations, creating an "us" and a "them" out of every single circumstance. Your history and your science are based on viewing the world through separation, and have taught you that your survival depends upon primitive instincts that cause you to respond in aggressive, competitive ways, rather than using cooperation and harmony to make your choices. You even believe that these instincts live in what you call the reptilian part of your brain, as if part of your brain can be separate from the totality of your whole self.

As you developed, you were given teachings through third-dimensional science and education that badly trained you to believe that those competitive instincts were the only instincts that exist. You have been incorrectly taught that aggressive and competitive behaviors hold the most value for your survival. You have been trained to believe that all of your instincts are based on a response to danger, and that something bad could happen to you if you do not automatically react with fearful flight, competition, or aggression to what you do not understand or what you *believe* threatens you. This, you call your survival instinct. If you focus only on *that* definition of instinct, you are missing a large part of Who You Are.

You have forgotten the spiritual instincts that are the more potent, powerful, and natural part of being human. We wish to help you to remember that you have a greater instinct beyond what your science has taught you. We wish to help you understand the true and real meaning of that larger instinct. From our perspective, your true instinct is what you were born with: your heart's awareness of human capabilities, your natural tendencies for cooperation, and your remembrance and awareness of Who You Are as beings of light and love. These natural instinctual aspects were taught and "talked" out of you through the bad training you have received. We will say more in a few moments about how your reality has been "spoken" into being.

All the possibilities that you have hidden away or forgotten still live within your hearts. Real instinct is not simply a matter of how you respond with automatic reactions through your autonomic nervous system. That sort of environmental response is only a small part of the totality of your instinct; you must remember how *all* of your instinct works in order to respond to your environment as fully functioning humans. The greater part of your instinct gives you the capability for balanced response within your environment, and the choice to *always* communicate and respond with love, rather than through fear. The choice to respond from a place of love to every circumstance awakens the deepest part of your instinctual heart-memory, reminding you that you will always be safe if you act from love rather than fear. Many of you call your intuitive ability to respond to the guidance of the universe within your environment your "Sixth Sense." We call this instinct your First Sense (described more fully in *Conversations With Laarkmaa, A Pleiadian View of the New Reality)* because it should be placed in primary importance above all your other senses. When you awaken your higher awareness and follow your true instinct, you will find that your First Sense (intuition or intuitive guidance) always points you towards your natural instinct to continually move towards peace, trust, love, joy, and compassion, for the highest good of all. This type of response will always ensure your survival.

We say that you can survive in any situation through using your larger instinct to guide you to act from your true nature, by simply paying attention, cooperating with each other, connecting with Earth, and being willing to receive the energy of universal guidance. If you pay attention to where you are and what is occurring in any present moment, it is impossible to be in danger, for you will always have inner guidance on what to do, and when and how to do it. You will understand what is required, and you will not have the need to compete with or get in the way of other energies that are not harmonious. You sense the energy of others and situations, either joining them instinctively, or simply moving away from them.

Our purpose in communicating with humans now is to help enhance your resonance with the truth. You must have a greater resonance with the energy of truth to begin to remember what you have forgotten. We have told you that infants arrive with their instinct fully intact; their First Sense and all of their other five senses are connected to the heart energy of love, which is connected to truth, joy, compassion, peace, harmony, and a desire for the highest good of all. They are connected to Source. The true nature of human beings lies in this energy of connection and heart-knowing. This is how humans arrive on the planet.

You must dismiss what you have been taught about your natural responses that relegate instinct to a lower vibratory realm, as if it is something to be overcome. You don't need to overcome competitive urges; you need to awaken to the spirit of cooperation and peace that is your birthright, and then competition will stop quite naturally. Your real instinct has to do with knowing and remembering Who You Are as beings of love and light who have the capacity to notice and cooperate in every present moment. Dismiss what your human parents, teachers, schools, science, and religions have told you about the necessity of competitive response in your third-dimensional world. Holding on to those beliefs that promote competition for survival only keeps you trapped in a world of separation and pain. Remember instead your natural instincts towards love and cooperation; those things that your society has told you are neither valuable nor real, are the *most* valuable and the *most* real!

As you begin to heal yourselves, you must remember how to utilize your true instinct. Begin by focusing your intention on your First Sense; become aware of it, use it, and you will have a better understanding of Who You Are, and how to better navigate your third-dimensional world.

The Energy of Speech

As beings who are waves of light (your etheric bodies) and waves of water (your physical forms are primarily made of water), you are very malleable. You are designed this way in order to interact with all available energies of the universe for greater harmony and creativity. When you arrive on Earth, you are still very fluid and connected to the energetics of your original essence. As children, you are very supple, mentally and physically. Your physical forms become more dense as you allow your thoughts to solidify into patterns of belief. As you get older, you add layer upon layer to those thought patterns, causing your physical forms (as well as your mental states) to become more and more rigid and dense, and therefore more challenging to change.

It happens like this: as young ones, humans must quickly adjust to a variety of sounds that are present in the third dimension, which is a very noisy place, full of creative potential. Sound projects the energy of your thoughts, causing the ripples that manifest into form. Sound is a prime creator, as we will discuss in more depth soon. As infants, humans understand the power of sound; you come here knowing how to use sound to communicate in order to manifest what is needed. Infants use the sound of crying to attract what they need. Infants use happy sounds to communicate the joy of connecting with other humans around them. And yet, even as you begin to understand how to use your own tones and sounds to affect your reality, you also begin to absorb the tones and words of others around you, some of which are positive (matching your natural state of joy), and some of which are negative (discordant, harmful, and unfamiliar to you).

As infants, you realize that others have been in the third dimension longer than you, and you notice that they have attached specific meanings to the tones and words that they use with you. As young ones, still so fluid and malleable, you easily absorb sound and tone, and you quickly begin to learn what meaning certain words and tones carry in your third-dimensional environment. As you begin to learn the meaning of the tones and words you hear, you are shocked to find out that so many words can be full of judgment. You didn't expect that. Many of these tones and words are negative and different from what you expected or remember from pre-birth. You may hear that you are good or you are bad, that you are beautiful or ugly, that you are clumsy or graceful, that you are smart or that you are incompetent, that you are right or that you only make mistakes. All of these words and the tones that you use fill you with meanings that come from the energy of judgment, blame, and separation. As infants, you do not know how to integrate such things that did not and do not exist in your other experience, and so you, too, began to separate and categorize everything as good or bad, right or wrong, in order to fit in with your new environment.

As these judgments of separation grow within your mental field, you begin to form your own beliefs to match the beliefs of others, making an internal agreement to be what you have been told you are. This causes a great shift, a great division within yourselves. It leads to a split between your hearts and minds. When that split occurs, your hearts no longer guide your thoughts, for you begin to guide your thoughts by the fear that you yourselves will be judged or that you are unloveable. You do not want to be wrong, for you are afraid that if you are perceived as wrong by others, then you will not be able to receive love. At first, you are afraid that someone else will judge you; later you begin to judge yourselves. Focusing on judgment of what is "right" and what is "wrong" according to the belief systems you have adopted, you use the power of sound now through your own words and tones, joined with the tones and words of others, to shape yourselves, often misbelieving the truth of Who You *really* Are. The pattern continues as you use sound to voice your own judgments about yourselves and others. This is how humans "speak one another into being" in the third-dimension.

But you are not infants or children now, and the patterns still persist, even while you are reaching to remember the truth about yourselves. It is time for you to look at the erroneous judgments you have accepted about yourselves, for those judgments have incorrectly shaped you into something that is not real. Then look to see how you force your own belief systems about what is "right" or "wrong" on others, particularly on your own children. Sometimes these patterns exist from generation to generation. Begin to examine and integrate the shadow parts of yourselves that you do not like, for this is where all of the accumulated wrong and undeserved judgments and criticisms lie unrecognized. These criticisms have caused you much suffering and separation. In order to heal from these judgments, you must begin to accept how they were formed, release them, and then begin to speak yourselves into higher forms with loving tones and words. Love and light always dissolve darkness, judgment, and fear.

It is now supremely important for you to notice the words and tones you use on one another, for the energy of those words and tones are creating your current reality. Pay attention to which words and tones come from fear, the ones that are full of separation and judgment. Pay attention to the words and tones that come from love, and notice how you feel the difference between the energy of sounds that come from fear and the sounds that come from love. Notice it all; pay attention to the sounds and tones you give to each other, and begin to realize how that simple action can transform the world.

Use your curiosity; don't be afraid to look beyond your

favorite beliefs and what you have been told is true by parents, schools, governments, religions, and most especially, by people that you love. Truth lives in your own hearts, not in what others say or the wrong ideas that have formed your belief systems. When you use your courage and curiosity to look at what causes you pain and to just *be* with and love whatever you find, you can begin to alter the separation and split inside of you that causes you to feel so alone. Humans have such a feeling of being divided, so split within yourselves, so separate from others and from Source in your current condition. Your chaotic separated beliefs and judgments cause you the pain of separation, making you feel discord and dis-ease. Through examining the beliefs that have caused you to feel judged and separate, you can rebalance yourselves and begin to heal all dis-ease.

Because we know that you wish to give your children the best experiences in life, you can begin to do this by understanding how you speak them into being through the tones that you use. Tones filled with kindness, acceptance, and love positively shape them into healthy human beings, while angry, judgmental tones radiate a message that they are not OK as they are. You must practice using words and tones that convey only the highest energies to your children. You must also show them by example, that not only will you not judge *them*, but you will not judge *others*. You cannot keep your children safe nor show them love by demonstrating judgment that causes separation. Teach them instead to discern and appreciate differences; help them to respond to and integrate varying aspects of energy, as those energies express themselves in both people and situations, rather than judging them.

Children learn about the third dimension through using *all* of their senses. Help them understand that what they remember from before birth in other realities *is* real, and help them to discern how *this* third-dimensional experience is different. One reason children reach to touch things that are hot is because they remember that they are divine flames, and they are attracted to the light. They do not understand that their new physical bodies cannot respond to third-dimensional heat or flames in the same way that they did in etheric form. As adults who know more about this dimension, you can use your tones and words to encourage them to safely learn about and respond to their environment here. In order to help your children adjust to and enjoy being in the third dimension, take them into Nature and enjoy together feelings of being at one with the natural elements of Earth. As you watch your children interact with Nature, you will begin to remember how to return to the natural rhythms that you have forgotten.

The Energies of Nature and Technology

Humans have aligned themselves with the rhythms of technology, moving further and further away from the rhythms of Nature. You cannot be healthy and whole when you turn away from and ignore Nature, for you are *part* of Nature. Most of you align your daily (and nightly) rhythms with the artificial speed set by technological patterns, only occasionally seeking Nature for a brief respite in your lives. It would be far more appropriate for you to align yourselves completely with the natural world and *occasionally* seek technological assistance as often as you now *occasionally* seek to be in Nature. The continual bombardment of your nervous systems with artificial stimulants (caffeine, sugar, television, the Internet, cell phones, and constant activity without balanced rest) not only damages your own delicate systems, it also damages the planet, for as we will explain later, humans are the neurological system of Earth. What you feel, Earth feels. When you "short out" your own systems, you are causing electromagnetic shocks to the earth. When you are calm, breathing in harmony with Nature at a slower pace, Earth responds with her own balanced rhythms. Most of the earth changes that are occurring now are happening *because* the irregular patterns and damage within your human systems are transferred into the earth. Earth operates under the universal law that everything is energetically connected. Humans continually ignore this law, choosing separation over and over again, blindly stumbling through life without conscious thought of how your actions, your thoughts, and your intentions affect all of life and all energies.

This is not the first time Earth and humanity have faced the devastating choice of Nature versus technology. Humanity's choice of technology over honoring the wisdom and power of Nature caused the annihilation of Atlantis. As the final technological explosion occurred, sweeping Atlantis under the sea, Lemuria was taken as well. The smaller yet more powerful culture of Atlantis had a detrimental impact on the larger, gentler society of Lemuria, which suffered from the poor choices of unnatural misuse and control of energy in the more powerful Atlantis. A repetition of the same patterns is emerging now through the choices of the elite in your more powerful and technologically-oriented cultures and countries. Those damaging choices are causing a path that *can* bring planetary de-evolution. The choice for de-evolution or conscious evolution is yours. Be wise in making your choice.

For thousands of years, humankind has focused on separation and competition, choosing selfishly without understanding that the harm you cause anything or anyone else also harms yourselves. Although technology *can* help you to connect, it can also foster selfish separation from Nature and from each other.

The illusion you have created through dependence upon technology has become so dense, it is experienced by most of you as reality. We wish to let you know that although you believe your technology is what you call "cutting edge," from our perspective it is quite rudimentary. The benefits that you *believe* you receive are not energetically balanced with the damage that occurs from the discord and electrical magnetic currents that bombard your physical forms. The speed at which you integrate your energy with the energy of your technology is not in harmony, and that perpetually increased speed accelerates your neurological systems, causing you to be continually tired and out of balance. Our technologies are harmoniously and energetically matched to our own natural rhythms and are life supporting. When you base your technology on principles that are against your own nature, it can do nothing but harm you and cause dis-ease. Pain and dis-ease are just warnings that you are out of balance and not living within the natural rhythms of the planet. You were designed to live within and act through the natural pace of both Earth and universal energies. The trajectory you have chosen through your misunderstandings of the correct interaction with and use of technological energies is taking you further and further away from a harmonious and balanced state.

While this may not be the first such choice humanity has faced, it is the *last*. You are facing the final choice point for humanity, with powerful energies arriving to support you to make the necessary choices to forever move away from separation and towards unity. Through making balanced and harmonious choices that benefit the highest good of all, you may bring forth the birth of a universal community that is re-harmonized with Nature and with the universal laws of love and light. Nature holds the wisdom that everything is connected. Your hearts remember that truth, but the separation of your minds from your hearts has caused you to forget that every intention, every thought, and every movement affects everything else. That is a universal law.

If you will only turn away from technology's artificial rhythms and return to the rhythms of Nature, you will find your way out of the denseness and into the light. You have reached the final choice point for humanity and the last changes the planet will undergo on Her path of ascension. (Earth is currently undergoing a process of change, which some call ascension, that will transform life on the planet.) Those who persist in living in density under the illusion of separation will find themselves in a golden trough of light, waiting to be transported to another world. They will perceive it simply as another round of karmic choices. Those who choose unity, love, and light, giving up all things that impede their progress, will move into the holographic form of a Rainbow body, with your light body and your physical form more deeply conjoined. Your lightness will cause you to ascend with Earth as She ascends. You will be the new humanity in Earth's Golden Age, and you will be able to use a higher energetic form of technology. It is a process that requires constant choice. Choose your use of energy wisely.

You are here now to integrate the energy of all aspects of yourselves, whether these aspects exist here now or in parallel lives. You must integrate all of your energy as thoughts, feelings, memories, or even physical challenges that arise within your awareness. Humanity exists now as broken puzzle pieces, scattered and divided through beliefs and opinions. It is within your power to join those pieces together into a beautiful picture of energetic wholeness. Everything that manifests now does so in order for you to take the pieces that have been broken, judged, and separated, so that you can love them, heal them, and join them back into the whole.

Begin within yourself and your own energy, for you are the *only* one who can heal *you*. You must first remember the divine light that you are. Begin by speaking yourself into a new form, using the sounds that reflect the energy of loving kindness, rather than judgment. Speak positive thoughts to yourself about Who You Are as a divine being. Then begin to use positive tones and speech with others in your environment. Speak to everyone and everything that you see with tones and words that come from the energy of love, so that each person can hear himself being spoken into the truth of who he is. Take such tones and speech into the world every day, dropping away from judgment, and speaking from higher vibrational energies of love. Such vibrations will come from your heart, and as you practice this, you will find that you are speaking yourselves into Who You truly Are. As you begin to remember, you will begin to heal!

Chapter Two

THE SPLIT OF DUALITY

"You came to Earth to experience the opposite aspects of duality, in order to learn how to harmonize them."

The Conflict of Opposites

The third-dimensional world is a realm of duality. You are here to experience the opposite aspects of duality and to learn how to harmonize them. Each experience you have in duality gives you a sense of opposites. As humans, you tend to polarize your own energy with one opposite or another in every experience. As you attach your preferences to one polar extreme or another, you create an energy of resistance between the two. That resistance causes the dynamic tension in which you live. You have done this for as long as you have been in human form, beginning with the androgynous split between male and female. Through your thoughts and beliefs about your experiences, you align yourselves with specific polar energies. The purpose of duality is to show you how to bring opposite energies together in harmony in order to merge them into one unified whole. You do not yet fully understand how to do this, for you do not appreciate the importance of the differing aspects of duality. In your current state, humanity has collectively decided that everything that is opposite *must* present at least some conflict, rather than being able to see the harmony in opposites and blend them together for a greater whole.

You have the general idea that opposites attract, and yet once the initial attraction begins to show any existing differences, the conflict begins. From our perspective, this is what happens: as each human approaches another human, you are initially attracted to the opposite energy you carry, but you begin to *notice* similarities. ("This person is like me.") After first recognition of your similarities, you then begin to discern the differences between you. Almost instantly, as soon as you meet, each of you wishes to express and increase your own energy, and convert the different and opposite energy of the other to match you in sameness. You begin to notice the other person as being "not like me." It is at this point that you begin to judge each other in a process of picking each other apart, causing challenges for yourselves, for judgment is the basis of all separation and pain. This tendency for judgment comes from a place deep within you where you feel you are not complete or whole as you are, for you have forgotten that you are connected to the universe and that everything you need is in your own hearts. What you feel in duality is in one sense correct: you are not complete and whole *until* you recognize and *remember* that you are divine beings who are part of Source. Yet you seek that wholeness in others, rather than understanding that you are already whole within yourself.

You come into your third-dimensional experience of duality, longing for unity, longing to be whole, and longing to be who you have forgotten that you are. That longing leads you to seek what you *believe* to be missing. You usually look to others to find what you cannot find within yourselves. As you focus on what you believe to be missing, you draw towards you the opposite energy of what *you* are expressing, and instantly you begin to feel more complete. You feel the similarity, which deepens your attraction to the opposite energy. Yet that completeness you feel from joining your energy with another person is false.

What you do not understand is that the opposite energy is only an expression of parts of yourself that you do not yet recognize, and so you are drawn to that opposite in order to see and remember that aspect of yourself. You are attracting to you parts that you have forgotten within yourselves. At first, this feels wonderful and you see only the similarities between you. You begin to experience the longing for unity even more, wishing to be more than you individually perceive yourselves to be. This is what you call "falling in love." However, once the opposite energy becomes more prevalent in your field, it becomes uncomfortable, for it stirs within you the remembrance that there is something more about Who You Are. As you notice the difference more and more, that difference becomes threatening and moves you towards greater separation. All of the lightness that was at first present in your relationship becomes dimmed and dulled by the layers of illusion that you put into place. And yet you still ask the other person to reflect back to you what she or he originally saw because you cannot see it within yourself. This kind of disillusionment happens in all relationships in the third dimension, and it is at this point that you begin to judge others more and more, sometimes even demanding that they provide what you perceive as missing within yourselves.

Two people who are drawn towards one another's opposite energy see something that reminds them of a portion of themselves that they remember from before. They remember a particular way of being that is not within their current dualistic experience. This is why opposites in gender attract one another. You see one another and remember the androgynous whole, and you yearn for the unity of what you remember. Yet as you begin to see the beauty of the oppositeness and begin to invite that experience together into a familiar sharing, the sharing often leads you into a place of wanting more from the other rather than awakening to the "more" that exists within yourselves. The "more" that you are looking for is a deeper connection and a greater remembrance of your divine relationship with Source, and the remembrance that you are whole and that you are part of divine love and light.

And so the dance of dualistic opposites is played in a game of conflict on this planet. Each of the two opposites begin to dance around each other, examining exactly what is different, for it is the difference that first draws your attention and then later makes you uncomfortable. This process polarizes you even more as you attach to the energy of those things you find familiar and comfortable, and begin to judge what is not familiar or what you do not like about the opposite energy. These energetic reactions further the separation that you are already feeling. What you need to understand is that the process we are describing is merely a function of dynamic tension occurring in order for you to have something to push against so that you may grow. The tension gives you the ability to understand that unity requires *both* aspects of duality working together to achieve a balanced harmonic whole. When you see something that feels like "not me," what you are seeing or feeling is an aspect of *you* that is not in embodiment at this particular time, and yet it *is* an aspect of you, for in unity, all aspects exist harmoniously together.

Since humans have begun to judge by thinking rather than discerning through heart response as you once did, you have begun to analyze your differences. You mentally decide how to change or improve an opposite energy, how to make the differences "better" (which is another way of saying "more like me"). You often seem to find it necessary to tell one another why your way is best and how the other could improve if they would simply change to your way of doing things! It would be much more helpful on your healing path to recognize and share with others your own divine gifts and talents, while allowing others to become more of who *they* are, rather than trying to coerce them into believing that your way is best. When you give of yourselves freely without expectation, you become more able to see and clearly align with what others have to offer because you are not focused on polarized beliefs that your way is best. This is a more harmonious use of duality that allows appreciation of and cooperation with polar opposites, rather than categorizing and separating each polarity as "right" or "wrong" through competition and conflict. Cooperation leads to unity;

competition and conflict lead you further and further into separation.

Look around at your world. How many of your activities, work, and even your games, are based on competition? How much suffering do you see in this system? How much dis-ease that needs to be healed? When you simply offer your own gifts and talents from a loving space without expectations of how others will respond, you free the energy to settle in resonance with those who are ready to receive it. The space of non-expectation also allows room for you to receive the gifts and talents of others. Cooperation within duality gives you the ability to see the *beauty* of dualistic polarities and to use them to create a unified whole.

Earth's duality is *a gift to you to help you grow*. Duality brings you the possibility of appreciating things that are different. When you are too hot, you appreciate a cold breeze. When you are too cold, you appreciate a warm fire. When you are too dry or too thirsty, you appreciate the wetness of water that quenches you. When you are longing for connection, you appreciate someone who can bring to you a reflection of Who You Are as part of the whole through their expression of oppositeness.

Humans were injected with fear thousands of years ago by forces that wished to control you. There is *no* power that can control you when you are unafraid and filled with love. However, because the element of fear was introduced into your systems, you have allowed that fear to separate you more and more from your memories of being divine, whole, and completely connected to the love and light of Source. That separation has caused you to look at anything that is not like you and try to make it *more* like you in order for you to feel comfortable and "safe." You feel safe in sameness, *even though that is an illusion*. When someone becomes more "like" you, the beauty of the dynamic tension that causes you to reach, stretch, and grow goes away, and you quickly become bored with the sameness, for you renounce part of what you were drawn to in the beginning.

Fear has been so strongly present in humans that it has deeply permeated your consciousness, and you have forgotten about your natural instinct always to return to love. When you surrender the fear that has been part of you for so long, you will understand how it has kept you separate and suffering. Before you were injected with fear, you always survived by understanding that you were part of Nature and through using your First Sense (your intuition) to guide you. You were safe and whole. Your First Sense directed you to act from your heart's wisdom through love, responding appropriately to each situation that presented itself. When you walk this planet without fear, simply discerning what is in your surroundings, there *is* nothing to fear. When you are not in a state of fear and you are in harmony with what is around you, you send out vibrations of peace that affect others in your environment as well, thereby keeping you safe. You create a peaceful kingdom where you will not harm others, and therefore, you will not be harmed.

Duality has been experienced for thousands of years as a march down separate paths, where people line up against each other and point fingers saying, "You are not like me; therefore I cannot trust you or love you." Begin to see each other as mirror reflections that reveal both your similarities and your differences as being the same, for you are literally parts of the same unified whole.

On this planet, duality exists as a way for you to utilize energy and to learn about energy in order to understand that everything *is* energy. With a greater understanding of energy, you can learn to manifest by blending all energies together. Being in duality is about learning to use the beautiful dynamic tension that is available to you to shape into form a more harmonic representation of unity. As you do this over and over again, you will open the boundaries between "self" and "other," eliminating the borders of separation. You will become more fully aware of, engaged with, and immersed in your different facets as part of the whole, freeing yourselves from the loneliness you experience in the third dimension. This manner of living moves you away from your habitual ways of thinking, feeling, seeing, and sensing in your third-dimensional world into a more multidimensional experience of possibilities, potentialities, and freedom. When you remove the veil of separation caused by your attachment to polarized beliefs, you will enter into the "All That Is." This is where you will find all that you are missing, and will experience the freedom that is possible when you accept everything about Who You Are and share it with others.

Symptoms of Duality

You have become so accustomed to the tension of conflict within duality that it feels as though this way of being is the your natural state. You experience everything in duality as separate; you categorize everything as "me" or "you," "self" or "other," or "right" or "wrong." The primary way you experience all energy is through separating it into these categories. There is some degree of separation in almost all areas of your experience. Although you are most familiar with this state of being, as you begin to remember how to use duality to reach unity, you may experience a sense of loneliness, reminding you that duality does not have to be so self-excluding and painful. When you notice an increased sense of longing for connection and an intensified loneliness, you are actually getting closer to the unity that you remember. To know that unity is *so close* and yet be unable to fully experience it deepens your sense of longing and separation. Many light movers are experiencing this intensified sense of separation in your families and communities, finding very little support for

Who You Are remembering yourselves to be. You are strategically placed around the planet to help others open to and begin to remember who they are as you express Who You Are. Your level of awareness, your pain from the sense of separation, and your longing for connection are all symptoms to show that you are beginning to remember, and you are evolving as you are designed.

Most of humanity in the collective "un-consciousness" do not feel the same great separation, for they spend all their energy in familiar patterns of judgment and blame that keep them attached to their polarized beliefs. There are also many humans who *do* feel the pain of separation, but distract themselves from what they feel. They are the ones who are afraid of looking at what they feel, and so they distract themselves through habitual and excessive use of television, the Internet, meaningless and trivial conversations, shopping, sex, alcohol, drugs, coffee, and other addictive substances that alter their natural rhythms. They use anything that will prevent them from slowing down to face the work of what needs to be seen and changed. These humans avoid the work of transforming separation into unity. It is those of you who so intensely feel the pain of separation who are seeking ways to change it. When you slow down and deeply listen, you can match your rhythm to the rhythm of the universe. You can then begin to sense the greater possibilities that are ever-present through love and unity.

As you develop conscious awareness, you may begin to feel *physical* symptoms of moving from duality towards unity. Your physical forms are not familiar with the energies and changes that are arriving on Earth to raise your vibratory consciousness and assist the ascension of the planet. Your light bodies, or etheric forms, are, however, familiar with these energies. Your physical forms, which have become quite dense through continued expression of certain thoughts and beliefs, are struggling to adjust to the influx of these new energies. Fatigue or feeling tired, not having your accustomed amount of energy, not resting at night, headaches, heart pains, electrical sensations, temperature fluctuation, and struggle with breathing, are some of the symptoms of moving from duality's conflict into the light of unity. Joining your etheric to your physical forms in a more connective way will enable you to more easily adjust to the changes that are occurring on Earth at this time.

You are etheric as well as physical, a light body *and* a physical form. Your physical body is struggling to adjust to the truth of Who You Are. That does not mean that the challenge will be too difficult, for you are greatly guarded and protected by guides and High Self Angels who carefully monitor how the new energies are received and absorbed, and the level of change that each of you can withstand in your individual physical forms. You will not be asked to tolerate more than your physical forms can bear. *Only* your fears and thoughts about what is occurring cause you any harm, for you manifest through your thoughts. We will speak more about this later.

Some of the symptoms you experience can be viewed from a broader perspective. For example, electrical pains in your chest can reflect the opening of your heart chakras. As your hearts begin to expand, you may experience an outward pulsing of energy in your chest, little electrical shocks, pressure, or pain as the incoming light pulses arrive. Such symptoms will not register on medical equipment, yet you feel them to let you know that your hearts are opening. This movement will only enhance your lives. Those who experience these symptoms are working very hard to join their physical and light bodies together. The accelerated pace of changing energies offers opportunities for you to do what you came here to do.

When you experience these physical "symptoms," many of you immediately begin to fear that something is wrong. Accepting the changes as developmental rather than pathological will prevent your overreacting in fear. The most important thing you can do at this time is to eliminate all fear, for when you are afraid either of the symptoms or the outcome, it impedes the progress of your evolution. Fear is the opposite of love, but it has no power unless you give it power. Love can dissolve all fear, so the path for your evolutionary movement requires you simply to examine any fear you experience, trust its purpose, and then send love directly into the situation. You may utilize your will to direct your thoughts towards love-based possibilities rather than fear-based questions about what is going on. Call on the assistance of your light bodies by always turning your thoughts towards potentials for development whenever you feel your physical bodies are struggling. Direct your thoughts towards gratitude; be thankful that you have the opportunity to move more fully into the higher vibratory being of Who You truly Are.

The Split Between Mind and Heart

We have been telling you how duality causes separation. The largest separation comes from your forgetting that you are one with Source. The second largest separation is the division between your mind and the wisdom of your heart. Your power is lost when you allow the split between heart and mind. You must utilize them both together in order to access your natural powers to co-create. The split occurs when you begin to allow your beliefs to govern your behaviors, rather than first listening to the wisdom that lives in your hearts. You begin to heal the split when you use your will to direct your thoughts through your hearts to your minds. In order to heal the split, you must learn to stop believing what your minds tell you from past experience, and begin to trust what your hearts have always known. Use your will to do this. Change *all* belief systems based upon past or future, and trust your hearts instead. Universal truth is always present in your hearts, and you can access it when you remove any fear that is in your minds.

One specific belief you must dispel is that you are victims of circumstance and that you have little or no control over what happens in your lives. When your hearts and minds are connected, the flow of universal wisdom is always available to you, and you can be powerful co-creators. When living in complete harmony with All That Is, you can manifest anything you want! If something arrives in your lives that you do not like, you must step away from your beliefs that you are either a victim or that you have no power to change it. Every circumstance is created by a combination of your thoughts and the flow of universal energies. You are fifty percent responsible for co-creating *at all times.* The universe is responsible for the other fifty percent. Your thoughts travel into space and are joined with other human thoughts and universal energy to co-create the world that the human collective focuses on and creates together. You can see from this truth why it is so important to release all thoughts that come from fear and turn to thoughts of trust and love, for those are heart-connected thoughts that give you the power to manifest a better reality for all. This allows you to heal the split between your minds and hearts, by utilizing your will.

When something happens that seems outside of your control, it is important to remember that your heart-connected thoughts have a fifty-percent ability to change the circumstances. Neither resisting nor resigning yourself to circumstances will change the outcome. Resisting what occurs only misuses your vital energy. Resignation only gives your power to those who may *wish* to control you. You must abandon any idea that you are ever victims. *You are not.* Things do arrive on your doorstep that can be uncomfortable, yet you have the power of choice to change your attitude about anything that comes your way.

Learn to recognize that everything is simply a certain arrangement of energy, and you have the power to shape that energy into something else by the choices you make. Change begins with your attitude and through acceptance of *what is*. You may then implement change by monitoring your thoughts about what is occurring.

You always have the power to co-create. Many things that seem challenging are for your highest good, intended to make you stronger and more resilient and to awaken you to your own powers. Apply discernment rather than judgment to each circumstance, utilizing your own will to direct your thoughts through your hearts. You can help shape any circumstance that is inharmonious or does not resonate with the energy of love, or you can simply love it until it dissolves. Stop believing *anything* outside of yourselves and learn instead to trust in your own hearts to guide your thoughts. We are asking you to radically evolve, quickly moving beyond your old thought processes. We are asking you to begin to trust that everything is unfolding as it should, and *you* and your choices are part of the unfoldment. The universe *is* supportive and harmonious. Remember that everything around you is energy, and you have the power to work with that energy to co-create your world.

Incorporating Duality into Unity

You know that your consciousness is moving towards unity. The time for seeing conflict in duality is over. You have experienced this for long enough. You know what it feels like, smells like, tastes like, sounds like, and looks like. It is familiar to you. You have the experience of conflict (*and separation*) well etched into who you think you are. The process of change allows you to remember and begin to heal your current condition. You must eliminate conflict at every turn, beginning with your own thoughts. When you find conflict within your thinking, find a way to creatively change those thoughts towards cooperation. Ask yourself, "How can I be creative and imagine this to be something more than what I *think* it is?" This is the beauty of using your attitude as a vehicle of change. Through under-standing how to use the energies of duality, you may change conflict into harmony, thus moving into unity. It is a process; you can draw this process out very laboriously step by linear step, or you can open your hearts to experience the process more quickly. Use the freedom of your imagination to help you stretch beyond what you think of as a static, hard, third-dimensional reality. Your imagination can help you create a more fluid, open, moveable, joyful reality that allows you to experience life as a flexible, dynamic, moving spiral of *multidimensional* wholeness. Your attitude can take you into the reality of joy and lightness that is your natural state of being.

In addition to using your imagination, a simple aware-ness of the energetic vibration of numbers can support your process. An excellent example of numerical vibrations, the Fibonacci series (the pattern that expresses in a nautilus shell, for example), is a mathematical system that demonstrates the energy of individuality as it approaches unity. The first two numbers in the Fibonacci series are zero and one (which add to one); each of the subsequent numbers is the sum of the previ-ous two numbers. For example, one plus two equals three; two plus three equals five; three plus five equals eight, and so on. As each set of individual numbers merges into a union, that union becomes an individual number standing beside the next individual number. Combining these two numbers once again forms another unified whole, so that there is a continual flow of separation moving towards unity. The Fibonacci series is a mathematical symbol of humanity's path. The discovery of the sequence was placed into your consciousness to help guide you

REMEMBERING WHO WE ARE

as one way to understand the movement from separation into unity. Use this understanding to help you see the similarities and move towards unity with everything that presents itself to you.

Dismiss all old training you have received that is based on separation. The concepts of duality as presented by parents, teachers, and other humans with whom you come into contact, have caused you to sever the cords of connection. At each place where you are severed from the truth, you begin to withdraw further and further into separation. This is why you have war, fear, greed, hunger, and all manner of things that you believe you must fight for in order to have your needs met. All of these things are based on your perception that there is not enough for all. As we have explained previously, you have been taught that only the most fit will survive through using competition rather than cooperation. This way of survival can only operate in a reality that is based on fear, a limited reality that requires you to compete rather than to cooperate.

In the true reality of trust, love, joy, compassion, peace, and unity, there is abundance of everything you need. This larger reality is based on the principles of cooperation and unity, for you have the knowledge within each of your hearts to *know* that there is always enough for everyone. You must begin to love and to help one another in order to utilize all the many gifts that are available to you. When you trust that everything you need is present and available, you will fall away from the patterned responses of competition that you call instinct, and instead you will open to remember your true instinct: that you *are* love, that you are here to trust yourselves and each other, allowing your hearts to lead the way. When your hearts guide you, you will remember how to connect with each other through simply setting an intention; your hearts, which work like waves of water, will broadcast your intentions, like a pebble sending out ripples on a lake. In doing this, you allow your energy to travel on loving vibrations, rippling out until it is received and acknowledged. It is important, extremely important, that you awaken to this understanding now! You are human beings operating in a third-dimensional world while *simultaneously* moving towards operating in multidimensional experience. What we are describing will assist you in achieving higher states of being.

All light movers are longing for connection now; all light movers wish to "go Home." You are tired of living in the tension of separation. You wish for some small token to show you that you are on the right path, doing the right thing, and that you are making a difference. From our perspective, you are here in human form doing work that shines the light of Who You Are into the denseness of the third dimension in order to bring the light from Home into *this* world. You are here to bring light. You do not need to wait to go Home. You are here to bring Home to the planet.

You are being given the great experience of choice here on Earth. It is a wonderful opportunity to feel the energies of duality and continually be able to *choose* your attitude, your thought patterns, and how you wish to engage in the world. It is through the element of choice that you can ultimately incorporate duality into unity. When you make *each* choice from love, you will have accomplished this. We wish to help you remember how to return to your heart's understanding of your natural instinct to move towards love, trust, joy, and compassion. Live by *that* instinct and help others remember how to live it. Remember, all humans are living on a planet based on duality and polar extremes. Duality will cease to exist as you bring the polar opposites into the harmony of unity by appreciating and accepting *everything* as being part of the whole and beginning to relate to it in a more balanced way.

Moving Towards Androgyny

The misunderstanding of the differences between the opposites of male and female genders has plagued your planet for thousands of years. We are devoting an entire chapter later to explain how and why you are androgynous beings. As you move more fully into your understanding of androgyny, you will remember that your experiences of being male or female come from choice. Explaining the concept of what androgyny means can be understood as knowing that you carry both male and female energies within each of you. Each of you has the benefit of being divinely male *and* divinely female within you. Through seeing the similarities of your genders, the dynamic tension of how you interact with one another will begin to lessen. Through your misperceptions of duality, you have allowed the polar extreme of masculine energy to rule over the equally important feminine energy. You have been out of balance from the original design of co-creative cooperation for far too long. The time for that is over; it is time for the feminine consciousness to lead both women and men, so that men understand that they also have feminine consciousness within them. Through the return of balance between feminine and masculine, the masculine will take its rightful place alongside the feminine energy to bring humanity back into wholeness. Healing the splits between the genders and between your minds and hearts that have been caused by competition rather than cooperation will speed you upon your evolutionary path.

Chapter Three

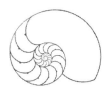

ASPECTS OF
THE THIRD
DIMENSION

*"Being in a physical body is a precious
gift that allows you to incorporate
the mental, emotional, and physical
realms for your evolution."*

Overview of Your World

We would like to share our perspective on how your third-dimensional world manifests. Because we wish to help you, we will speak about your perspectives and your dysfunctional patterns from many vantage points, often repeating the same truth in different words. The third dimension is made of these basic components: the mental realm, the emotional realm, and the physical realm that you see and touch. Remember, each of these realms is merely an aspect of energy. You relate to each of the mental energies through the aspects of beliefs, judgment, competition, and your misconception of time; the emotional aspect helps you understand your relationships to everything; the physical aspect is a reflection of your etheric energy as it manifests into physical form through your relationships with food, drink, thoughts, and words. We have focused on these concepts, making this is the longest chapter in our book. The reason for this focus is that *you* focus most of your awareness on these aspects of the third-dimensional world. Additionally, this is the area that holds the most potential for change. There are many other realms available for your consideration outside of the third-dimensional world, and we will address these later in the book.

We will begin our exploration with the mental realm, for the mental realm is where your intentions are formed, and this is where your thoughts can create what comes next. Your mental realm is mostly full of beliefs, thoughts, and judgments. The mental realm is also where you have created time. Each of these facets is combined together, along with the emotions, to create your third-dimensional reality.

Because of the split between your minds and your hearts, the mental realm currently causes great separation in your world, for you continually create things without having a focus or an understanding of *what* you are creating through your chaotic and undisciplined thoughts. Through your thoughts, you have separated everything into categories of time (past and future) or judgment (good and bad). These categories of separation are hardened into a dense physical reality through your beliefs. Beliefs are not the same as what you *know* through the wisdom in your heart, for what the heart knows is always based on love. Beliefs are based on how you categorize your experiences in your mind or on what you have been taught to believe by others (school, religion, family, colleagues, and peers). Beliefs comprise a specific limited system that holds your thoughts within that system. If circumstances fit within the system of your limited beliefs, you feel comfortable, for they are familiar to you. If something unfamiliar occurs outside of your particular system of understanding, you often categorize it as foreign, unacceptable, or "not good." You then separate yourself from it in order to maintain a structure of beliefs within your comfort zone and a false sense of safety.

Humanity has misunderstood how to use the mental realm. The mental realm is best used for discernment of differences in order to harmonize those differences. The way your physical world is reflected begins with the thought process in your mental realm. But you have confused your mental energy, adding emotion to discernment, thereby creating judgment, which keeps you in a form of separation. The proper order for thinking is to direct your thought with your will through your heart to your mind. You hold intentions as energy when you turn them into thoughts. How that energy is used is up to you. When you power that energy with positively oriented feeling states through the use of your will, channeling all thoughts through your heart to your mind, then you can begin to manifest your physical reality in accordance with what you truly need and want. Later we will speak about how you can better use your mental realm to co-create your physical reality by using your will to focus your thoughts, directing them through the heart before they are released into space to create form. So far, humans have not completely understood how to do this.

The second aspect of the third dimension is the emotional aspect. First you must know that emotions are not the totality of your feeling state. Your natural feeling state is comprised of joy, trust, love, compassion, peace, abundance, safety, and harmony. Emotions are the part of your feeling state that reflect imbalance. These imbalances are experienced as feelings such as sadness, anger, frustration, grief, jealousy, and greed, all of which stem from the largest emotion of all, fear. Your emotions are intended to help you understand and balance your relationships with everything.

While our evolutionary path was distinctly different from yours (for we do not have emotions), we *do* understand quite clearly and directly that any evolutionary path to expanded consciousness has belief systems that must be transcended, no matter which species is evolving. We may not have experienced emotional pain as you understand it, but there was pain in our own evolutionary process as well. Part of your evolutionary process is to redefine how you use emotions.

You are currently creating physical states that are mostly dominated by the realm of your emotions. You were never intended to use emotions to create your physical reality. They are intended to point out how you are out of balance and to remind you, through the discomfort they bring, that you have stepped away from the *true* reality. When you learn to use your emotions, as we will explain later, they can guide you back into your natural feeling states so that you can co-create what you really want and need in life through love and acceptance rather than through fear and chaos, which never bring you what you *really* want. Emotions are gifts; they are signposts to show you how you are out of harmony and what is needed for you to bring yourselves back into balance. It is *your* responsibility to pay attention to and follow the guidance of your emotions in order to correct imbalances within yourselves.

In your current human condition, you focus your awareness on *feeling* your emotions, without knowing how to *utilize* emotions to rebalance yourselves. Currently emotions are poorly understood and mostly misused. You misuse emotions to express what you are feeling but do nothing to regulate that feeling state to bring it back into harmony. You simply notice that you are having an uncomfortable feeling, and then you attach that feeling to negative thoughts, thereby creating judgment, blame, and separation. Through *this* process, you create all manner of chaos with an immature and undirected release of energy. In other words, you use the drama of your emotions as an escape valve, or what you call "venting" (ranting and raving), that *always* spills onto others, rather than taking the responsibility to use your emotion to guide you to understand and correct what is not working in your life.

When you mature as human beings and learn to use your emotions to rebalance your feeling states and use your will to direct your thoughts, your capacity to co-create a more positive reality with the universe will increase. With maturity, you will gladly utilize your emotions as signposts to show you how you are out of harmony, and you *will* take responsibility for self-correcting, rather than allowing ungoverned emotions to link with poorly directed judgmental and blaming thoughts, thereby creating more separation in everything you experience. Most of you choose to blame others for what you are feeling, rather than taking responsibility for and acting on the guidance emotions bring you. Your emotions come from within *you* to show you how *you* are out of balance in the way you are responding to or interacting with others or with circumstances. You must begin to realize that it *is never* and *can never* be someone else who causes you to be emotional.

All feelings from your natural state (love, trust, joy, compassion, peace, abundance) exist within your hearts. Your emotional states of fear, grief, anger, greed, frustration, jealousy, and sadness exist only within you as a combination of tangled, inappropriate thoughts that are attached to what you *think* about what you are feeling. Emotions can direct your energy back into harmony whenever you become separated from your natural feeling states, if you observe and take responsibility for them. How you attach your thoughts to what you feel determines what is manifested in your physical reality. This is why it is so important to link your thoughts with your hearts, where your natural wisdom lives, so that you can manifest a world of harmony. Your physical existence is actually a manifestation of combined energies of thought and feeling or emotion, reflected from the etheric into the physical.

We have explained in detail in our previous book, *Conversations With Laarkmaa: A Pleiadian View of the New Reality,* how the etheric form acts as a mirror and reflects the image of your thoughts back into your physical body to manifest your form. It is important for you to understand that the etheric (your light body) is a living, real, energetic essence. It is affected strongly by what you think and what you feel. It can only reflect wholeness and health into your physical forms when you unite your hearts and your minds, using your will to direct your intentions to create from a positive space of love and light.

As you become more adept at harmonizing your thoughts and your feelings, the cells of your bodies expand, and your DNA opens, allowing more dynamic life to enter you. In other words, you become healthier. Your physical bodies are conscious workspaces where you may follow the guidance of your emotions, and use your will to direct your thoughts through your hearts.

We will now repeat and expand upon the aspects of the third dimension so that you may begin to integrate a higher level of understanding. This is a tremendous amount of information for humans to integrate. From our perspective, it is appropriate that you begin this work now and accelerate your understandings at an energetic level, not only at a mental level. We will supply energy to you as you read these words to support your under-standing so that you may *remember* how to use your thoughts, emotions, and physical bodies to support your journey into higher consciousness.

The Mental Aspects of Time and Dimension

In your third-dimensional reality, you focus most of your attention on the mental plane; what happens to you is filtered by how you perceive it. We wish to help you return to the understanding of unity by correcting your misunderstandings of time, belief, and judgment.

We will begin with the mental aspect of time. *There is no time.* It only exists for humans through the Veil of Illusion that you have created through separating your experiences into categories, and through your forgetfulness. In other realms, it is known that time does not exist, for in a unified field there is no need for categories of past, present, and future. They all exist simultaneously. From a perspective of unity, you can clearly see that everything is connected. You invented time because you have no concept that everything is happening at once. You lost this understanding, or "forgot" how unity works, when you separated your thoughts from your feeling states. When your

44

hearts no longer guided your thoughts, all sense of connection ceased, and you moved into separation. This original separation caused you to divide your experiences into separate intervals and create the illusionary structure called *time*.

One of the major time-related erroneous beliefs you must correct is your perception of actions through the concept of cause and effect. In your linearly based third-dimensional reality, you establish patterns of behavior that are linked to time. You believe that if you do something a certain way, then you can determine the outcome based upon prior experience *every time*. When you *believe* that by taking a certain action, something *predictable* will follow, you are locking yourselves into a reality that can only have one particular outcome. Such limited thinking eliminates other possibilities that may contribute to different outcomes that are equally right, or possible. We are trying to show you how your misconceived notion of cause and effect is an old and limiting paradigm. When you move beyond your linear focus, the concept of cause and effect has no place. In multidimensional experience, you can no longer rely on any particular action as having the same effect each time it occurs, because the energies of each situation are different. Each experience is new unto itself, which completely eliminates the concept of cause and effect as a base of reality.

Humans have a great misunderstanding of cause and effect that largely comes from accumulating and storing your experiences into categories of the past and future. Fear and judgment have created beliefs based upon what you have learned from "history" or what you *believe* will happen in the future. You *believe* that you only learn from the past, rather than understanding that you learn in *each* present moment as it presents itself to you, for each moment is unique and offers a new possibility. The key to making the most of every possibility is to approach each moment with your full attention, allowing yourselves to live in the timeless experience of *now*, where there is no accumulation of pain, fear, or beliefs based upon perceptions of past experience.

We will speak about parallel lives, which we defined in our previous book, to demonstrate our point. By categorization of events through the mental construct of "time," many of you think of your experiences from other lives as "past" and refer to those experiences as "past lives." You even consider that you may be experiencing karmic effects of those "past" lives now in this one. Actually, in the true reality, you are experiencing all of your other lives, which we call "parallel" lives, at once, simultaneously, but your *attention* is focused only on the life you are conscious of currently. Your parallel experiences represent various aspects of Who You Are, which exist *in other dimensions.* Those experiences are not past, for past does not exist; those experiences are *parallel,* existing *simultaneously* with your current experience.

As you begin to remember that everything is connected, you will have the opportunity to integrate all of those parallel experiences in your current life. In fact, you have the opportunity in the particular energy you are living now to harmonize *all* parallel lives at once to heal the divisions within you and move from a limited, third-dimensional experience into a liquid, multidimensional experience. In the process of this integration, you may experience what you think and what you feel more potently in each moment, for you will be collecting the energies of all of those parallel lives *simultaneously* in order to balance and integrate them into the completeness of Who You Are becoming. As your consciousness is raised, you will begin to integrate into one healthy and whole human being. If you can understand parallel lives as aspects of yourselves existing in different *dimensions* rather than viewing them through the lens of *time,* you will have a much clearer understanding of Who You Are.

Imagine yourselves standing in the middle of a room surrounded by twelve doorways into other dimensions. Each of these doorways represents an entry point or a portal for looking into a different dimension in which you exist simultaneously. Look around at each of the doorways and open one; look at the individual aspects of yourself in that particular parallel life. Looking at these aspects opens you beyond time and separation into multidimensionality. You have many, many parallel lives, extending into infinity, existing as multiple dimensions. What you remember about other experiences that are not part of you in *this particular* lifetime are parts of Who You Are; they exist in parallel dimensions. Understanding this concept will help you to remember that time does not exist, but parallel dimensions *do* exist, for space is inclusive of *all* dimensionality.

The third dimension is limited by your interaction with the false idea of time. What you need to understand is that there is no real basis for thinking or believing that there is a past, present, or future. In order to really grasp how you are capable of joining with Source to co-create a better world, you need to step away from this restrictive paradigm and begin to understand that everything happens simultaneously.

If you choose to separate events into artificial categories of an *imagined* past or future, you are robbing life from the very *real* present. You choose to create and give life through your thoughts and emotions to an illusionary past or future, creating an artificial reality: *time.* You therefore lose the potency of the *now.* The *now* is all that is truly real and is the only place where true manifestation is possible. The past and the future are illusions that you create through the energy of your thoughts; those illusions cloud the realization of now, causing a continued, complicated, and chaotic manifestation in the third dimension. If you wish to manifest something positive and real, you must focus on change in the present moment. The power of change lies only in the present, not in the past or the future. Only the present is real, and it is the only place where change *can* occur.

Some humans have believed *time* to be a fourth dimension, thinking that it exists as another aspect outside your third-dimensional reality. Your creation of time keeps you bound to the third dimension. Time is not a linear fourth dimension existing beyond the third dimension. Because you think linearly, you believe that time must exist in a linear progression somewhere beyond your current third-dimensional reality. *We have told you that time does not exist.* Remember that time is merely a construct of structure that humans have agreed upon together. When you engage with your concepts of time, you constrict your ability to enter into and participate with multidimensionality. Remove time completely, and you will exist in the field of a multidimensional universe comprised of All That Is. When living fully in All That Is, you can manifest anything you want!

The illusion of time only enhances your sense of separation. Ignore your former training about time as past, present, and future, and begin to look beyond those concepts into the existence of simultaneous experiences in varying dimensions. Expand your thinking and learn that believing in time actually blocks you from experiencing multidimensionality.

The energies available for you now are opening you to a larger experience in order for you to *remember* that you are multidimensional beings. As you begin to experience yourselves in this way, you will open to possibilities that are beyond your wildest imagination. For instance, if you remove time completely, you will be able to *instantly* communicate with one another. If you remove time completely, you will be able to *instantly* transport yourselves to any place in the universe. If you remove time completely, you will be able to experience omnipresence, being in multiple places simultaneously. Cullen remembers the truth of this reality and calls it "Zip Zip Zip!" This expanded awareness is a large part of what is necessary for healing the human condition and helping you to remember Who You Are.

The Mental Aspects of Belief and Judgment

Humanity exists now as broken puzzle pieces, scattered and divided by random thoughts and conflicting and erroneous beliefs. It is within your power to join those pieces together to create a beautiful picture of wholeness. We wish to help you correct how you currently use your thoughts to form beliefs and judgments. Your mental realm has become clouded because you have allowed your emotions to attach to your thoughts, rather than using your minds for simple discernment. We will speak more about the emotional realm later, but for now, know that if emotions are attached to thoughts, your thoughts become beliefs, and your discernments become judgments. Judgments lead to blaming others rather than taking responsibility for changing yourselves. Your minds wish to retain your dualistic perspectives, because that is how you make sense of and try to control the third-dimensional structures of your experience. Old patterns have quite a tenacious grip on human minds, and your minds *always* want to be in control. The mind rules through duality and separation; don't you know this? The mind was *never* intended to be the guiding force for human beings. The heart was designed for that purpose. There is great separation in humanity at this time between what the heart *guides* you to do and what the mind *directs* you to do. The evolution of consciousness is about reuniting your hearts and your minds. We suggest that you stop focusing on the mind as your most important organ. Your minds will quickly lead you astray, because the mind *always* wants to be in control—always, always, *always*.

When your minds attach to an emotion and accept it as a certainty, you form a belief. This is what happens when your thoughts arise spontaneously without connection to your hearts. Don't believe what we say, for we also are outside of you. Only trust what is in your hearts. *Belief* is different from *trust,* because trust relies on your heart's inner knowing and is connected to feeling states of joy and peace. Belief is formed from thoughts that have been separated into mental categories based upon prior learning or experience. Each of you is harmed by your own beliefs about what occurs in your life. You choose your own dis-ease according to what you *think* and *believe* about your experiences. Through the influence of your beliefs, you begin to change discernment of differences into judgments. Discernment becomes judgment when an emotional reaction to something challenges your beliefs. A simple discernment of differences becomes a judgment when you attach your emotions to your thoughts.

Judgment is one of the major elements of your mental state that causes separation. It can also be seen as one of the major toxic factors in causing dis-ease. If you judge others, you have no room to love them. Even though you have been taught that you should not judge one another, you still do it. Judgment seems to be one of the most *difficult* patterns for you to break because of your levels of fear. The powers of fear causing separation are deeply ingrained within you, and they emerge as judgment. The idea that you should not judge is a mere mental concept to you, something that is spoken and written, *but not lived.* You are so immersed in judgment as a daily activity that you do not understand when you are doing it, how it creates toxicity within your environment, and how it affects your psyches and even your physical bodies.

To heal the human condition means that you must heal the proclivity for judging yourselves and judging one another.

When Christ said, "Judge not, lest you be judged," he meant that every time you judge, the energy of judgment will harm not only others, but will also come back to harm you. Through judgment, you create a lower vibratory state that causes dis-ease. If you wish to heal the human condition, if you wish to be whole, healthy, functional human beings in your true divine state, you *must* cease judging all together.

In order to heal, you must learn the difference between discernment and judgment. We repeat that discernment is *simply* noticing that differences exist, while judgment attaches emotions through your belief systems to the differences you perceive. In duality, it is neither possible nor desirable *not* to discern differ-ences. In other words, you must remain alert and use your observational skills to notice the differences, however slight, in everything. How could you notice the beauty of the different flowers if you could not discern their differences? Discernment is always appropriate. It is the attachment of emotions to your discernments, thereby turning them into judgments, that causes the conflict that can lead to sickness and dis-ease. There is no judgment present in noticing whether a flower is yellow or red; both are beautiful. There need be no judgment when you notice differences between each other either, because each of you is also uniquely beautiful.

The key to determining whether you are discerning differ-ences or whether you are judging one another is to check and see how you *feel*. When humans move from discernment into judgment, there is *always* an emotion present. If you experi-ence any emotion, you have stopped discerning, and you have moved into judgment. The moment you begin to judge, you begin to generate toxicity within your own body, and you extend that toxicity into the field of others, as you pass the energy of judgment to them through your thoughts, your tones, and your words. Those on the receiving end can feel the toxic vibration of judgment as it permeates the entire environment. When you think judgmental thoughts or make judgmental comments, you are emitting a toxic energy into the collective consciousness, polluting the collective with your harmful thought forms. You must take responsibility for what you bring to the world through the vibrations that you choose. Judgments carry a negative energy. When you attach them to the comparisons you make of others, you are separating yourselves from each other, as well as generating a toxic world.

Belief systems feed judgments. You must learn as a species not to rely upon old patterns of belief. Learn to walk away from what you perceive as history. History has no meaning, for as we have told you, *time does not exist.* You may argue that you learn from past experiences. For instance, you may know from experience not to burn your hands on a stove, but we would say, if you put your hand close to a stove, your First Sense will tell you not to touch it. You do not need experience to guide you in the present. It is a fallacy for humans to think that you learn best from *past* mistakes. Each opportunity that comes to you is an opportunity in the *now,* and relying on an illusionary past does not necessarily affect the present. Instead it keeps you stuck living in old beliefs, preventing you from listening to your hearts and what is happening in the current moment. The only thing that has meaning is the present moment and what is happening *now.* Your intuitive sense will guide you towards what is appropriate in *each* moment of now. Learn that beliefs are solely formed from past experiences and release them to be fully present in each moment.

If you *believe* that the way that you can do something is better than the way someone else can do it, notice that there is an emotion attached to your belief. That belief leads to you to judge the other person. When an emotion is present, you must work to dissolve your belief, release your judgment, and open to the possibility that the other person is simply exploring a different way. Wish them luck in their exploration; perhaps they will discover something that they can contribute to what you know. If you have trouble with this concept, question why you believe your way to be better. Remember that discernments notice differences in order to harmonize them, while judgments are attached to fear, causing separation.

Most of you have a self-protective mechanism that supports your beliefs and keeps you separate from one another. Your beliefs come from tired, old teachings based upon competition rather than cooperation, and they cause you to continually participate in judgment. We want you to understand that you can *never* decide what is right for another person, no matter what you *believe.* Each person has something to learn and something to contribute. If you have doubts about this, question your heart and see what *feels* right. When your heart tells you something is correct, do you follow what your heart tells you? Always check with your heart to see if your thoughts are correctly aligned with love. Learn to release the many old beliefs that have been ingrained in you in this and many other lifetimes.

If you wish to heal the human condition, you simply *must* move away from patterns of blame and judgment. From our perspective, both are forms of abuse. Abuse in any form only promotes discord, disharmony, and dis-ease. Whether you are abusing yourself through self-judgment or abusing another person through blame, the same energetic harm occurs as if you were actually striking yourself or another person. This is an abusive use of energy and affects all relationships. How can any abusive relationship be healing? Abusive relationships cause lack of self-confidence, dampen the immune system, and ultimately cause so much distress that dis-ease occurs. What do you think you are doing when you are blaming yourself or another? You are simply abusing yourself or the other person.

The tones that you use to communicate and the thoughts that you think can be either loving and kind or harmful and abusive. Think loving thoughts, or stop thinking. Always stop your current thought process and start over again. Use tones of peace and love when you speak, or do not speak at all. If you express what you want to say with angry or overly emotional tones, you abuse yourself first through sending out that energetic vibration to your etheric form, and then you abuse others in your environment as they receive those tones. If you do not honor and respect what you are doing through the thoughts you choose, the tones that you use, and the words that you speak, you will continue to have discord in your relationships and cause dis-ease.

We have watched you for a very long time, and noticed that you cling to blaming and judgmental behaviors when you can simply make better choices. Humans love to whine. You blame and judge others to support what you *believe* is right without taking responsibility for looking at the places in your own lives that are out of balance. The amount of energy you focus on thoughts that contain judgmental and controlling beliefs determines how much dis-ease you experience. Wake up, humans! If you wish to heal, wake up and move into Who You truly Are. Remember that you are light beings who have no need to blame or judge. Your healing will not be complete until you can fully participate in life by removing your own dysfunctional thoughts, beliefs, judgments, and actions, and step fully into trust.

Competition or Cooperation?

Your third-dimensional world has predicated its values on competition, which can only exist when you judge one another. From our perspective, your beliefs that success can only be attained through a linear progression, where you must be "higher" in your achievements than others in order to realize success, have caused you to continually act through what we call "hierarchical competition." Such belief systems are based upon judgments about yourself and others. The action of judgment is fed by your strong desire to compete, which stems from an ancient fear that there is not enough for everyone. You may even have a sense of pride or ego about doing something well because the sense of competition has been trained into you at a *very* deep level and at a *very* early age.

We wish to speak about your sporting events, your academic competitions, and your competitive nature in a way that may shock and surprise those who believe that competition is healthy. People align themselves with sporting events and teams, wanting *their* teams to be "number one" because of a sublimated sense of personal failure in their own lives. You seek the exhilaration of a "win" for your team in order to feel good about yourselves. Because all humans are accustomed to making continual judgments, you have a misguided sense of what actually engenders success. Success can only come from recognizing that each human is a part of you, that you are part of each other, and that you are all the same. We use the word InLak'Ech, which means, "I am another yourself," to describe this understanding. Dividing yourselves into groups and teams that compete with one another only serves to further separate you. Moving towards unity requires eliminating competition and beginning to cooperate by recognizing and appreciating the gifts each of you offer; you must look for those gifts rather than judging others to be deficient if they do not match qualities that you personally judge to be of the highest value, or rather than competing to prove that you are "better" than anyone else.

It is time, as you move past the conflict of duality into a new season of unity, to set aside all notions of competition, and to adopt the concept of cooperation instead. Simply stop competing, and stop teaching your children to compete. Teach them instead to hold their hands out to one another in gratitude and cooperation. Teach them to look for and honor others' gifts that may be unnoticed or completely different from their own. Teach them that when one person has a gift, it should be offered and shared with others. Teach them to cooperate with each other, rather than judging that they are better than or less than one another. Bumper stickers that parents and grandparents put on their cars proclaiming that their child is the smartest, the best athlete, the most special, or "number one," further reinforce a competitive spirit that deepens the existing sense of separation. How do you think other children feel who never achieve this "special" status or whose own gifts and talents are ignored or dismissed? Do not promote competition through sporting events, intellectual evaluations, bumper stickers, or anything that says that you are "number one."

You must understand and help your children understand that the *actual* energy of the number *one* is only a starting point and should not be considered as being at the top. Only in the third dimension through your competitive dualistic beliefs is being "number one" considered the same as being the best. In the greater reality, it is known that the vibration of the number one is a starting point, a place of igniting, not a place where you finish because you have achieved something. *You have it backwards.* You usually think of number one in terms of competition rather than in terms of the energy that the number *actually* expresses. You are confused about what you are encouraging when you teach your children to aspire to being "number one" in either sporting events or intellectual pursuits. While trying to be the best that *you* can be does not involve judgment, trying to be the best at another's expense *is* acting out of judgment. Acting through competition comes from a place of being fearful that there will not be enough, that you will not be loved, or that you will not get what you need if you are not the winner of the competition. Teach your children with comments such as, "Yes, you have done well. Now how can you help another do well?" and "What and how can you learn from someone who did it differently?"

It puzzles us why loving parents would wish to instill such competitive values that actually prevent a child's ability to *always* feel safe and loved. Dear Ones, we tell you that competition is *never* something that can be won. There can be no true winner from competition, for competition causes harm to *everyone*. The one who loses has a poorer sense of who he is, and the one who wins has a *distorted* view of himself, with a false and empty sense of superiority. Winners know that winning is always temporary and that they must prove themselves over and over again. This knowledge instills even *more* fear within them, as they work to continue winning in order to maintain their distorted sense of self-worth.

Winners and losers in any competition are separated from the whole, through assigning values of being either the best or not being good enough, causing a disruption in the flow of unity. Either way, there can be no winners. It is a fallacy to continue to believe in this competitive way of life. Step away from your sporting events, and invent new forms of cooperative play for your pleasure! Do you not know that most of the events in which so many of you are involved are merely acts of aggression against one another? How can such choices do anything other than increase your sense of separation? These destructive patterns of behavior are also affecting Earth. We notice that your species has a tendency for aggression in almost anything that you pursue. If you are not engaged in aggression and competition with each other, you often act in an aggressive manner towards Nature and Earth. Choose to find something where everyone can join and be equally and non-competitively a part of the whole, rather than aggressively competing against one another.

The quality of gentleness is an antidote to aggression. Aggression is not part of unity; it causes separation and harm, both to the aggressor (although it is not always immediately obvious to the aggressor that they are receiving harm from their own aggressive actions), and to those with whom they compete. Taking advantage of others through aggression can never bring you success, whether your aggression comes through an emotional, financial, or physical act, or through the use of power. Winning through placing another at a disadvantage is not winning anything at all. Those who participate in these competitive behaviors are actually judging themselves as well as those with whom they compete. Through their own judgments, feeling that they must get better and better, they cause themselves greater separation, often bringing about more and more dysfunction and dis-ease.

Humanity is ingesting the toxicity of your competitive thoughts and actions on such a daily basis that it is no wonder so many of you are dying from dis-ease. Judgment has become part of your daily diet. On a regular basis, you swallow the concepts that you must compete in order to survive, and that you must be better than someone else to be acceptable. You mistakenly believe that there is something wrong with you if you do not participate in competitive pursuits. Such beliefs cause permanent dis-ease within your mental bodies, which are aggravated by unbalanced and uncorrected emotions. This imbalance then translates to distress in your physical bodies, often creating actual physical illness. When you attach unresolved emotions to your competitive thoughts, you create more permanent patterns of dis-ease that transfer into your physical forms. All of the fears and manifestations of fear and judgment that are characterized as anger, grief, jealousy, greed, and frustration are locked within the cells of your body, keeping you in dis-eased states.

Do you not know the cause of cancer? The cause of cancer is judgment. It is nothing more than that. It is quite simple. All the billions of dollars that you spend to find the cause of cancer will not bring you the cure until you eliminate judgment, for judgment is the *root* cause of *all* dis-ease. This is a profound truth. *Judgment causes dis-ease.* What you call cancer is one of the greatest dis-eases of judgment. Many diseases can be traced to acts of judgment. Consider heart disease. Most of those who suffer from heart disease are *dis-heartened* because they judge themselves too harshly, or they *feel* unloveable from being judged by others. When someone suffers from judgment, either against themselves or judgment from others, there may be enough judgmental energy to cause an imbalance that may present itself as heart dis-ease.

Look inside of yourselves. We implore each human who is hearing or reading our words, to examine your own emotions and beliefs. Every time you observe that something is different from you, please notice if you experience an emotion. Trace the emotion and find the thoughts that feed judgment. Every time you judge, you create toxicity within your own system, so you are virtually poisoning yourselves. Would you choose to eat or drink something that you knew was poisoning you? (Many do: they choose cigarettes and alcohol and sugar. So we know that some of you make these choices even with the knowledge that such choices will harm you.) Some of you do not know that you are making harmful choices for yourselves and others when you judge. You may keep clean diets, abstain from drinking alcohol or caffeine or from smoking cigarettes or taking drugs, and yet unknowingly, you ingest the poison of judgment on a daily basis, for you do not have the understanding that you have a choice to do it differently.

You always have a choice. Please remember that humans *always* have a choice. You have a choice not to eat certain things, not to drink certain things, and you have a choice not to *think* certain thoughts. When you notice that others do things differently than you do, you have a choice to pay attention if emotions arise, and if they do, to take responsibility for redirecting your thoughts, and to step away from judging, so that you do not poison yourselves or others. It is within your range of choice to do this, choosing health rather than dis-ease.

When Christ spoke of not judging, he was speaking of not poisoning others and not poisoning yourselves. We agree that it is not helpful to poison yourselves or others. This is not simply a spiritual tenet to follow if you are on a spiritual path, however; *this is a universal principle of manifestation*. If you are judging, you are manifesting toxicity within your energetic field, your emotional body, and your mental body, and all of those toxins will impact your physical body. As you reflect negative (or positive) energy into your etheric body, a manifold return reflects to your physical form. If your lives are full of judgment, you will be susceptible to dis-ease that can manifest into diagnoses such as cancer, heart dis-ease, diabetes, colds and the flu, and many other forms of physical dis-ease; you *will* have dis-eases that come from judgment because of your choices.

It is impossible to compete without judging your competitors. And so you must drop competition and judgment in order to heal. Now is the time to gain understanding of how you have been making choices that create dis-ease and begin to choose differently. If you wish to heal the human condition, if you wish to stop all illness, then you must stop judging and competing with one another. We cannot be plainer than that.

The Emotional Aspects

We have defined emotions earlier in this book, as well as in our previous book. It is very important for you to know the difference between your natural feeling states and your emotions, and to remember that the purpose of emotions is to guide you back into harmony when you are out of balance. They are to be used to remind you of the *true reality* and Who You Are. Nature and harmony flow with the universal energies of love, joy, trust, and compassion, which as we explained earlier, are *not* emotions; these are natural states of being within the universe. Your natural state has been eroded by a toxic environment, in a world of duality where you have been trained to look at opposites through an attitude of conflict and competition, rather than with cooperation and appreciation. An environment of constant competition promotes a continual fear that you are not good enough, and a fear that if you are not good enough, you will not be loved. This type of faulty thinking can do nothing but poison humanity.

The state of love and acceptance is a state of non-toxicity, a state of being in flow with Nature and the universe. Your natural feeling state lives within your hearts. Feelings from your hearts guide your relationships, for they teach you how everything is connected and related. When you are feeling love, trust, harmony, compassion, peace, and joy, you are aware of your *true* nature and your connection to all. When you are feeling emotional discomfort, you are removed from your natural sense of unity. Do not allow emotions to lead your response to life. Emotions are meant to show you places of disconnection within yourself. Each time you judge something or someone, your judgment stirs your emotions in order to guide you away from judging. Emotional states are *always* uncomfortable, for they are not within the flow of Nature and harmony. These uncomfortable feelings are there to show you how you are out of balance. Learn to recognize that emotions are simply energy; they are both your energetic gift and your energetic responsibility.

When humans become emotional, they are expressing a

reaction to something that they experience. If that experience involves another, you then believe that it is *the other* who causes *your* emotional reactions. Most of you suffer from the illusion that your emotional responses are about *others'* behavior, when they are actually about how you are personally reacting to what is occurring. *Others are not responsible for what you feel through your emotions.* It is an illusion to believe that others can make you feel reactive. The truth is that what you feel is your responsibility *alone*; it belongs only to *you*. No one else is responsible for your emotions, nor can anyone else return you to your natural feeling state of love and peace. Every time duality shifts your perspective in order for you to learn or grow, the proper use of emotions will bring you back into balance more quickly. When you accept responsibility for how you feel in any given situation, your emotions can then serve to return you to harmony. Remember, only *you* can choose how or what you feel, for your emotions belong only to *you*.

When you make choices while you are experiencing emotion, your ability to choose appropriately is clouded by the emotion. Because humans often make choices based on their emotions, those choices are neither clear, crisp, or in flow. We suggest that when you are experiencing an emotion, you ask yourselves, "What am I thinking?" The connection between your thoughts and feelings must be made clear. Taking responsibility for your own feeling states and using emotions to guide you back into harmony leads to discernment rather than judging. Thus you begin to properly use your emotional guidance, taking personal responsibility to work with your emotions. When you do this, you are healing the split between heart and mind, becoming more healthy and whole. This is what we call shadow work, requiring courage and dedication. Shadow work can be defined as the process of examining and beginning to love and change all of those aspects of yourself that are either blocked in your conscious awareness, or that you do not feel comfortable with or like.

Many of your negative thoughts are attached to emotional states because you do not know what to do with the uncomfortable emotions that you are feeling. You want the uncomfortable feelings to go away; you want to quickly rid yourselves of any discomfort. Often you distract yourselves from what you are feeling or else you blame someone else for what you are feeling. This is when most people revert to addictive behaviors to mask what is making them feel this way in the first place, leaping headfirst into the illusion that it will go away if they ignore it. Have you noticed that this doesn't work? The only way to get rid of an uncomfortable feeling is to take responsibility for it, to fully feel it, and live that experience without any judgment about what is occurring. Look to where the emotion is pointing, stop your thoughts immediately, focus on your breath, and breathe in the four essential elements of love, trust, joy, and compassion. In this way, you bring yourselves back into harmony. We will expand more fully on how to do this in Chapter Five.

Begin to examine your emotions through your hearts, rather than simply following old thoughts about what you are feeling. Allow the emotion to show you how you are out of balance. When you feel an emotion and use your minds to search for a historical reference that could possibly explain your discomfort, your thoughts will always focus on some *story* about what has occurred. By incorrectly focusing in this way, you assure yourselves that you will find *something* or *someone* to blame for your own feelings of discomfort, anger, sadness, or fear. Your minds will try to find specific incidents or imagined causes outside of yourselves, rather than allowing the emotion to simply show you what pattern *you* need to examine about your own life in order to change. The seed point of change is always found within quiet listening, and *then* choosing conscious thoughts and actions.

We tell you, Dear Ones, your distress is always *yours* alone, and nothing in your environment or any other person can cause you to feel distress. It is only *you* that can cause discomfort within *yourself*. It is only within *you* that emotions arise to teach you about yourselves. As you feel an emotion arising, listen to the wisdom of your hearts, rather than engaging in habitual patterns of negative thinking. Humanity needs to break that pattern. The correct way to use your emotions is to experience the full range of what they offer without becoming personally attached to them or seeking any meaning outside of yourselves. Stop thinking about what may be causing "the problem" when the emotion arises. Blame does not help humanity to heal anything; blame only darkens and separates. Thinking is best accomplished when emotion is absent, not when emotion is heightened. You can never think clearly when an emotion is present.

You often choose to connect your thoughts to disruptive emotional patterns because they are familiar to you, even though they may not serve you. You choose to give vent to your emotions because you *think* that expressing them makes you heard or seen. That is not necessarily accurate. It is important to honor and respect what you feel, and then move through it, but to fall into a familiar emotional place only *because* it is familiar will not help you to change your circumstances. Western concepts of psychology, with which we strongly disagree, have trained you to voice your emotions, or to speak to others about how you feel. Through this inappropriate training, you have learned to avoid responsibility for what you feel, often blaming others or circumstances outside of you. Blame and judgment of others will not help you. This pattern encourages victimhood and takes away your personal power. You must *own* your emotions and use them as your personal tools for change. Do not allow your emotions to rule you, but rather let them show you the work that you need to do to improve your lives.

We call working with emotions your shadow work. Shadows are the parts of yourselves that you are often afraid to see because you are afraid that they point out how you are not perfect. You can only be perfect through being willing to love and accept *all* aspects of yourselves. You must be brave enough to look at your shadows within your personalities in order to bring them into the light. If emotions lie unacknowledged, they will eventually arise to be resolved, demanding your attention and interfering in the flow of your lives. They cannot remain suppressed in the shadows indefinitely. It is best to examine your shadows to see what needs resolution, and use your emotions to guide you. It is through working with your shadows that your emotions can direct you towards the freedom of being full and complete. As you work with your shadows, you become more aware of your emotions. You can and should use these emotions to guide you back into harmony repeatedly, as you release old beliefs and patterns of thinking.

Remember, you can meet anything that comes to you. You can handle whatever is in your path. The lowest emotional vibration is fear, and it is fear that keeps you locked into separation and pain. The highest vibration is your feeling state of joy, which leads to and is an expression of unconditional love. It is the vibration of joy that is the key to opening all of your DNA. Laugh, for laughter adjusts your vibration. Being grateful, laughing, and focusing on beauty makes a difference in your energy. Be grateful for everything. Follow the guidance of your emotions to heal yourselves and return to your natural feeling state.

Our last comment about emotions may surprise you. Because you are accustomed to experiencing so much pain in your lives, you are often magnetically drawn to focusing your thoughts on your suffering, rather than heeding pain's signals of imbalance and beginning the process of change. Healing is about moving away from dis-ease and back into ease. The way to do that is very simple; *difficult* but *simple*. The reason you experience dis-ease rather than ease in your lives is because your thought forms and belief systems are so complex, and you so often attach your emotions to your thoughts. You may not be aware that because your thinking has become separated from the guidance of your hearts, your thinking has become too complex for your ease and comfort. When you focus on whatever is causing you dis-ease or discomfort, you prevent your return to the balance that sustains you. When you focus on love, you will always find your way towards unity and flow. Healing is about continually re-finding your balance. Your emotions are there to help you.

The Physical Aspects

We have explained to you how the mental and emotional elements affect your physical forms. What we want you to know is that *everything* you do affects your physical bodies. The physical world that you experience as human beings is a wave of accumulated vibrations that you have called into form through your thoughts, your emotions, and your actions. We have spoken in great detail about how your emotions affect physical manifestation, and in even greater detail about how your thoughts affects the physical. We will now give you guidance on how to heal your physical bodies by examining not just what you eat or drink, but *all* of the things that affect your physical forms, including your thoughts and actions.

The first thing you need to know is that you have created a story about the physical body through your beliefs about how life and death occur. Most of you believe that all life ends through the process of physical death. We would like you to understand that physical death is only one pathway to reach a multidimensional state. Each of you has the choice to change your form through death, or to change your form by joining your light (etheric) and physical bodies together to create a fully functioning multidimensional state, which we call your Rainbow body. To create a Rainbow body requires a process of making conscious choices in every present moment. We call *this* process the true form of ascension. Choices made out of old dysfunctional habits and old beliefs that match the beliefs of the collective unconsciousness of humanity, lead to the process of death. Conscious, aware, and responsible choices lead to ascension into Rainbow body form.

Intense energies are arriving on Earth now to support you in making wiser choices. These energies support your ability to release your many unconscious beliefs and old patterns of behavior. With clarity and an open attitude, you may begin to make choices that support your own path for ascension with a Rainbow body, rather than choices that lead to physical death. We suggest that you begin to consider *everything* from a multidimensional perspective, rather than from your limited third-dimensional viewpoint. Start by looking at what you eat and drink.

We will begin with a refresher on your diet, starting with your choices of what you eat or drink, and then expanding your awareness to help you understand that what you ingest goes beyond food and drink. This is important because everything that you ingest affects whether or not you will be capable of ascending into multidimensionality and changing into Rainbow body form. The energy of what you eat and drink moves into your etheric body. The etheric body reflects back that energy to shape and form either a healthy or a damaged physical body.

We suggest that you eat a living, *vegetarian* diet. If you eat animals that have been killed, you are making a choice to change your own physical form through death. You are aligning your physical body with the energy of death, while *believing* that you are supporting life through what you eat. The energies that support physical life and the energies that support physical death are contradictory. Do you wish to make choices that lead you to death rather than choices that lead you towards living in infinite space as expanded forms of love and light? Do you wish to be considered by the universe as primitive cannibals? If so, continue your habitual comforts and beliefs that you must eat meat in order to survive or to feel "full."

You will never be fully nourished by eating something that has been killed. Even when you *believe* that the killing has been accomplished with kindness (such as the humane caring for animals that will be killed or kosher killing), it is still taking life away from a living being that is connected to you. You are connected to everything; that means that you are connected to every animal that you eat. If you take an animal's life, you take part of your *own* life. Additionally, when you eat an animal, you ingest the fear that animal felt when its life was taken. If you are ingesting dead animals, including fish and fowl, then you are ingesting the energy of death, and you are choosing to change your *own* form through death.

The faulty belief that you must kill to eat comes from a competitive viewpoint, rather than from a perspective of cooperation and unity. These dysfunctional beliefs and actions fail to support you on your evolutionary path. You have the opportunity to make higher vibrational choices for the greater good of the whole. We strongly suggest, although it is always your choice, that you immediately stop killing animals for food. Killing simply continues your illusions and your experience of separation. You cannot support life with the essence of death.

The next thing we would like to discuss is sugar. Sugar is one of the most toxic physical substances on your planet. Even though it is produced from one of Earth's natural plants, it is *not* a naturally occurring earthbound substance. The idea of processing sugar cane into sugar was brought to Earth by beings that wished to keep you ignorant of universal truths in order to control you. Sugar is a substance that is used to lower your consciousness, keeping you in addicted states and under the spell of fear, and it is harmful to you. Those who taught humanity how to make sugar do not wish you to expand, awaken, and remember the power you carry within you. You often believe that a sugary treat will make you feel better when you are stressed. It will not. Because of its addictive qualities, you may *temporarily* feel an artificial boost when you eat sugar, but the effect quickly reverses into negative consequences.

Sugar has jagged edges that rip your DNA and tear holes in your light body. It does not matter if the sugar is derived from sugarcane, sugar beets, evaporated cane juice, or sugar from corn syrup; it is all damaging. If it is sugar or a closely linked substance, *do not eat it* unless you wish to give up your own power and be controlled by others. The ingesting of sugar (which most humans do) prevents the connection of all twelve strands of your DNA, and prevents your being able to function as you were designed. You were originally designed to develop by utilizing all of the aspects available through connecting your twelve strands of DNA. By including sugar in your diet, you cannot manifest a full and healthy physical form, and you certainly cannot ascend in a Rainbow body status.

What you call "fruit sugars" are *not* sugar at all; they are Earth's natural sweetening agents, and they are beneficial to your bodies. You may also eat naturally occurring sweets from plants and trees (stevia or birch bark) or from the bees (honey), for those sweets are also compatible with your systems. You may even include small amounts (in balance with other things you eat) of maple syrup or rice syrup, for these substances do not upset the glycemic index in your digestive process, unlike agave, corn syrup, and sugar. This means that these preferred substances enter your system slowly and can be easily assimilated without spiking your insulin levels. But remember, Dear Ones, that the sweetness you seek in life was never designed to fill the empty spaces that you may be feeling or to distract you from the work you are here to do. You cannot fill those empty spaces by eating sweets (or anything else). Those empty spaces exist to remind you to fill yourselves with the sweetness of love, and they can never be filled by artificial sweets such as sugar, or by any other kind of comfort foods. Nature intended that you accept Her sweetness in a harmonious way that is balanced with other things you ingest. Sweets should only be included as part of a complete nutritional package, not for the sake of their sweetness alone.

We would also recommend moving your diet towards a larger percentage of living green foods and foods that alkalize your bodies. Because plants easily replenish themselves, you may ingest their gifts without taking their lives. Choose to ingest plant-based proteins and green drinks, rather than relying upon meat and grains, which are highly acidic. Acidic foods lead to dis-ease because your digestive systems are not designed to process such material. Eat vegetables, sprouted or soaked beans, and nuts, adding fruits on occasion as appropriate. Maintain a balance between *lightly* steaming these foods and eating them raw, according to the needs of your individual systems and seasonal conditions. These living foods support health because they are alkaline in nature, while most of your usual foods, which are acidic in nature, do not. Limes are an excellent food for maintaining an alkaline balance in your systems. We strongly suggest that you rebalance your diet to include a predominance of green and living foods.

Now that we have discussed food in depth, we wish to focus your attention on the importance of what you drink. The most important thing you can drink is pure, clean water. Both you and the planet are mostly comprised of water; without drinking adequate amounts of water, you cannot keep yourselves in balance. It is important that you ingest only *pure* water, not water that has been contaminated by human treatments that render your water undrinkable (such as adding toxic chemicals like chlorine and fluoride). Water is a primary source of nutrition. Water, along with light and love, gives nourishment that supports your physical well-being as you move towards multidimensionality. When you drink water, we suggest that you place your hands around the glass or container of water and hold it to the light before you drink it. Ask the light to combine its energy with the water; also combine energy from your hearts. Do this each time you drink water. When you do this, you will simultaneously send healing energy into the waters of Earth and all of the people on Earth, as well as ingesting water in a more nourishing form yourselves.

While water is the optimal drink for humans, we need to address other substances that you drink. Bottled fruit and vegetable juices contain no nutritive or enzymatic value because they have been processed and stored. Drinking these substances is of no real benefit to the human body and provides a false sense of satisfaction. Simply drinking pure water is of much greater value. Similarly, carbonated drinks cause distress because the carbonation process (adding carbon dioxide to the drink) creates air, which when ingested, disrupts the natural process of the digestive system, placing undue stress on your kidneys and your liver as well. Carbonated soft drinks present a double problem for you. They contain both sugar (cane or corn syrup) and carbonation. You already know the detriments of sugar, so with this combined information, you can make your own decision about what you are choosing to drink.

Alcohol and drinks that include caffeine are the most damaging choices that you can make in your drinking preferences. They are equally damaging for your physical bodies in opposite ways, for both contain either artificial stimulants or relaxants that prevent your bodies from being in natural resonance with Earth rhythms. Ingesting artificial relaxants and stimulants affects your entire neurological system and is abusive to both your physical and emotional well-being. You often rely on caffeine to boost your energy to an artificially accelerated rate of activity. Then once you become overly stimulated, you rely upon alcohol to slow you down. Alcohol numbs your neurological systems to the point where you are no longer in rhythm with your own body, the earth, or the universe. Continually engaging with these substances will eventually short-circuit your entire neurological makeup and cause dis-ease. Believing that you must have caffeine to start your day or drink alcohol to unwind are dysfunctional beliefs that you need to reexamine. After all, do you really want to spend your lives in artificial states that leave you tired and disconnected?

Nicotine, recreational drugs, and many pharmaceuticals are also artificial stimulants or relaxants that alter your brain function and natural rhythms. You harm yourselves by using these substances to force your systems to match the artificial and dysfunctional rhythms to which you have become accustomed. Many, if not most of them, are designed to make you *believe* you can function more easily and successfully within your society. Actually, their use keeps you separated from your natural flow and from remembering what you are here to do. These substances impair your natural ability to listen, preventing you from hearing instructions from the universe, and they cause you to focus on the Veil of Illusion that keeps you stuck in an artificial third-dimensional reality. Wake up to be more in resonance with the planet by using Nature's own pharmacopoeia of healing substances, and rejecting all of these harmful and disruptive man-altered agents. (*Please work with your doctor, and use your own common sense to make healthy choices.*)

If you wish your physical forms and light bodies to resonate and merge to create a Rainbow body, make the choice not to eat or drink the artificial things we have described to you. Return to the natural rhythm and harmony of life through ingesting only natural substances. Allow your heartbeat and your breath to return to the rhythms that are in direct harmonic resonance with Earth and the universe.

There are other elements that you must consider, as their energies also affect your physical forms. Artificial rhythms created through the use of technology, such as television, cell phones, and the Internet, affect your physical bodies through their impact on your neurological systems. All of these things speed up your brain function to an unnatural and unsustainable pace. We understand that you currently use these technologies for communication, but we suggest that you use them more sparingly, rather than so constantly. While we are happy to share with you better and more effective ways to communicate, you will find no space to learn about them, if you habitually rely *only* on receiving information through technological means. Use these tools more sparingly rather than making the Internet and cell phones your main ways of communicating. Spending more of your time in Nature will restore your natural rhythms. We are not suggesting that you abandon technology altogether, but rather that you rely upon it less and less. Attachment to third-dimensional technology only keeps you stuck in the third dimension and prevents the development of abilities to communicate with one another in more natural, meaningful, and joyful ways.

What you ingest in thought, tone, and word is even more important than what you eat or drink. Pay attention to what you consume through sound, tone, and vision, including the thoughts you think, the way you express those thoughts through tones and speech, what you watch in movies, or the violence and negativity you consume through watching the news. Watching or listening to violence tears your etheric forms and expands the energy of fear, which then reflects into your physical bodies. If you ingest violence, drama, and fear, you will eventually manifest a fragmented, separated, fearful, dis-eased, and dysfunctional physical body.

The energies that are available to humanity now are much more potent than any energy ever experienced on Earth before. Because the physical body is unaccustomed to these powerful energies, you may at times feel out of balance, even while making healthy choices. Do not assume that there is something wrong with you. Instead, greet these energies with openness, curiosity, and the understanding that they are developmental rather than pathological. Just because what you are feeling is unfamiliar does not mean that there is something wrong with you or that you are ill. The experience of multidimensionality comes in *waves* that are designed to elevate your vibration, in order not to overwhelm you by arriving all at once. Fifty percent of the opportunities for raising human vibration comes from the universe. *You* are responsible for the other fifty percent. Pay attention to each energy and use conscious thought, conscious intention, conscious tones, conscious speech, and conscious actions to raise your own vibrations. Through doing this, you will learn how to manifest healthier and more functional physical forms for yourselves.

You are primarily nourished by Source through light, through water, and through love. You can only *truly* be nourished by aligning with your purpose and the work you are here to do as beings of love and light. Sound (tone through sound), light (reflected through love), and water (waves of movement), are the primary energies of manifestation. Learn to heal your physical forms by integrating and utilizing these primary energies for your nourishment: light (love) and sound (as it moves through water in the physical or through waves in the etheric.) Humans are experiencing great transition right now. We ask you to focus your thoughts on how you are expanding and co-creating a different way of being. You are already beginning to experience these new waves of energy in your physical forms. Accept and integrate these energies while you alter your physical diets and begin to change your thoughts. As you incorporate these energies and release your *beliefs* about what is necessary for your sustenance, you will find that you do not need such dense physical foods. You may even find yourselves moving towards more liquid diets, as you become more and more wave-like in moving towards the formation of your multidimensional Rainbow body. This "light" diet that we have suggested will lead you towards being sustained and nurtured by the sun's light, the light and love you share through your hearts, the pure water that increases your abilities to move in wave form, and the sounds that help you to resonate with higher vibrational frequencies. This diet will support your evolution as you continually move towards more harmonious states with yourselves and others. You are healing the human condition with our assistance and the assistance of all others from love and light. You are returning to your connection with Source through accepting that you are divine light and love. Remember that you must take your own personal responsibility through using your courage and will power to make these changes happen.

Sexuality

One of the things you have misunderstood the most while living in duality is human sexuality. In fact, sexuality has *mostly* been misunderstood and mistreated by the majority of humans for a *very* long time. You are made of water and light, which may be seen as a combination of water and fire. Your sexual experiences were intended to help you understand how to use your fire and your water to merge in unity through sharing your hearts and bodies, where you can experience the expression of complete joy and love. This can only be done in the safety of a committed relationship where two people have agreed to share all of themselves with one another.

A special condition is reached when two such people combine their electromagnetic elements of fire and their elements of water together, causing a reaction of alchemical union. Sexuality was designed to cause this alchemical union through uniting the hearts of two people as they interact with one another in a unified field of energy. It is through divine sexuality that you can give and receive unconditional love without hope or expectation. Through the expression of your sexuality, there exists a place where each participant can experience giving freely without the need for receiving anything in return. This is a special place of meeting one another without any *need* for personal gratification or release. This meeting is a powerful place of energetic exchange at the highest possible level.

Humans always seem to be looking outside of themselves for love and fulfillment, rather than realizing that they have everything they need within themselves, and that they can share it with someone they love. Most human sexual experiences are entered into for individual sensation or individual pleasure (which is an act of separation rather than movement towards unity), without the free-flowing exchange of gratitude, bliss, and joy. Most humans cling to sexuality because of their need, believing that they will be filled with everything they *think* is missing or incomplete within themselves through the sexual experience. They demonstrate outwardly loving behavior while holding a desire to receive something in return.

Our explanation of sexuality goes beyond your biological understanding of sex for reproduction. We are explaining how you can use your sexuality to reach unity in a way that you have not yet experienced. Divine sexuality *needs* to be understood in a completely different light in order for you to reach the place where you can use the fire of your electricity and the magic of your water to create the alchemical mix of unity in an energetic act of love. True divine sexuality cannot be reached without understanding three things: the giving of oneself, the ability to completely surrender in order to fully receive another, and the expression of communication through shared heart resonance. To freely give of oneself requires giving without expecting anything in return. Complete surrender removes all barriers in order to fully receive. This kind of surrender cannot be reached without a deep sense of safety within the relationship. You cannot find the absolute safety required for surrender without complete and total trust in one another. This kind of safety and trust can only be reached within a loving relationship where each partner is committed to the highest good for both of you. What we are describing can never be attained through casual sex.

Complete trust in one another leads to a shared heart resonance. Heart resonance is not only a *real* form of communication, it is the *ultimate* form of communication, for it shares the total energy of Who You Are with the total energy of who someone else is in order to enhance both of you. Humans rarely achieve this advanced and loving form of communication, and yet this form of communication is the true purpose of your sexuality. Everyone can reach this divine form of communication when you openly share yourselves as we have suggested. When you merge your fire and water together in complete love and trust, you then understand unity.

The Physical-Etheric Relationship

We will speak in detail about the etheric soon, but for now the basic truth you need to understand is that the relationship between the etheric and the physical is crucial to your health.

The etheric carries a perfect blueprint for the physical, yet that blueprint receives damage from the impact of your unresolved emotions, negative mental thoughts, and the improper substances you ingest in your physical bodies. The etheric body can retain scars from those encounters, leaving a scar in your etheric field. Such scars create imperfections in the manifestation of your physical bodies. An etheric scar caused by repetitive negative thoughts, an extreme upheaval, or constant emotional outbursts, can cause weak places within your physical bodies.

Emotion is a very powerful human element, more powerful than most humans realize; utilizing positive intent and positive thought forms rebalances your feeling states and helps your etheric bodies to create and enhance your overall physical health and well-being. The use of positive thoughts coupled with positive feelings has the potential to heal etheric scars so that you can create a more balanced third-dimensional physical body.

The physical body that you inhabit is the manifestation of your consciousness. This physical body is your workspace. It is within the consciousness of physical form that you have the opportunity to transmute darkness into light by clearing all your shadows and eliminating all residual states of fear, and it is the physical body that allows you to make overall growth in every aspect of yourselves. It is *extremely* difficult to make the necessary adjustments for your evolution if you are not in a physical body. It is important for you to understand that being human and possessing an actual physical form allows the space for this work to take place. The human form is the *only* place in the universe that provides this kind of opportunity for this work to happen.

Universal energies are now present to support the acceleration of your human evolution. You are experiencing many energetic opportunities to release yourselves from the prison of your beliefs and old patterns of behavior. These opportunities arrive to help you remove emotions that have become stuck.

The veil of separation from Source that you created is so thin now that humans may repair etheric tears through the application of proper thoughts. Some days more universal energies are present than on other days, creating increased portals of opportunity for growth. The energy of these days may be perceived simply as waves or ripples to assist you in breaking patterns, old patterns. On these portal days, your experiences may feel more intense. These waves of energy offer you an opportunity to move closer towards being wavelike, as we are in our form. Waves are always more fluid and vibratory, which enables them to more easily encompass change. We are waves. Humans are waves pretending to be static, solid particles. It's time to lighten up, Dear Ones! Honor the connection between your physical and your etheric to become more flexible, fluid, changeable, and able to transcend any circumstance that comes your way.

Moving Light

You call yourselves "light workers" without really understanding exactly *how* it is that you can "work" with light. We prefer to call you "light movers," for it is through moving *in* and *with* light that you make changes. In order to be effective as a light mover, you must understand what that entails. To be a light mover, you must bring light into the denseness of physical form and use it to raise the consciousness of your entire being and the planet Herself. As liquid crystalline fluid, your bodies provide a space for changing darkness into light. It is through your bodies that you learn what is truly important and how the pain of judgment and separation through thoughts and actions manifests into physical pain. Physical or mental pain invites you to move light into the rigid patterns that you have created to hold all of your fears; those fears are locked within the cells of your bodies and have kept you in a dis-eased state for far too long. Accepting and working with pain in all of its forms encourages you to remember that you are fluid beings with the power to change anything by working in harmony with the universe. You have fifty percent ability to co-create your circumstances, as the universe provides the other creative fifty percent.

Everything that you create in your physical bodies is formed by the energy of your thoughts, which move from intention energy, through your hearts into thought energy, and finally into the energy of physical form. The physical body is the most important resource that you have to provide the opportunity for a direct experience of the repercussion of your choices. This is why your experience of pain is a gift: it alerts you to something you are choosing that further separates you from light. Your bodies process fears into the manifestation of your shadows; your bodies process the dissolving of those shadows through the movement of love and light. This is why we call you light movers.

Once you learn how to move light within and through the consciousness of your own forms, you can then extend the light that you are out into the world, bringing more light to the creation of form on your planet. It is a precious gift to have a body with which to work, to have a conscious form that is willing to undergo such suffering in order to transmute denseness or darkness into light. The more you realize the magnitude of this gift and work with gratitude, the quicker the changes will occur. Do not focus on what is painful, but rather on what has *caused* the pain. Find the point of separation from truth in order to heal and transmute it, and the sensation of pain will transform into joy as you move light towards it.

When you complain or continually voice the negative, you are not moving light, you are accentuating the dark; those voiced negative thought forms actually increase the density of what you are already feeling. When you judge anything (or everything), the power of sound through voicing those judgments and negative thoughts causes another layer of denseness within your form, and simultaneously sends out an energy that causes *more* separation and density into the world external to you and beyond (to others and the planet). When you use tones and words from love and light, the physical consciousness responds, and you begin to feel lighter and lighter because the darkness and heaviness of judgment has been removed.

As we have already suggested, it would be wise to learn to monitor the thoughts and words you use with *light* continually, so that you take advantage of the gift of being in physical form. Periods of silence can help to break harmful patterns. Use intentional silence to remind yourselves of the power of sound when you do begin to speak. Use the calm created by silence to gather and project your thoughts before you speak them. Then bring your consciousness from the peaceful silence to a higher vibratory level by using only words and tones filled with kindness and light. As we will further explain later, sound carries the power to manifest. As you practice this consciously and consistently, your suffering will stop, and your pain will turn into joy. Your physical consciousness will be more capable of melding with your etheric light bodies through lightening its own density. *This is important.* This information is of great value in being a light mover.

All light movers are suffering greatly in varying ways at this time. When pain and suffering appear, you must not become negative about whatever challenge greets you. However life moves in the swirling patterns of change around you, the one thing you do have responsibility for is your attitude—always. You are most negatively impacted when you allow unresolved emotions and negative thoughts to surface in response to what happens in your lives. Recognize and take responsibility every time that you find yourselves out of balance, and simply rebalance yourselves. Your attitude is your power. By remaining positive, you can eliminate the effects of any darkness you may encounter; you can keep yourselves protected from any danger; and you can heal yourselves from anything that is out of balance.

Use love and compassion to make a difference in your own vibration and to raise the vibrations in your environment. You cannot laugh and be angry at the same time, nor laugh and be in a bad mood at the same time. If you are laughing, love and light are right there. If you are laughing, you are entering the space of joy. Darkness cannot affect you unless you allow it to through your own thoughts and emotions. Negative self-talk enhances the negative vibration in the field around you so that dis-ease can enter your space. You prevent dis-ease by meeting everything that comes to you with love. When you greet all energies in this way, you have the power to send them away if they are not resonant, or to join the universe in changing them through the power of unconditional love.

Even though you may sometimes feel lost, you have more help than you know. *You are light movers.* Your guides may become less obvious to you as you become more adept at moving light. They wish for you to stop relying on anything outside of yourselves for answers; they wish for you to awaken and remember that the wisdom and power for change live in each of your hearts and are within your own grasp. It's time to figure out how powerful you are. Every conscious choice you make determines how quickly you evolve into being able to use your own power. As unfair as it may seem, Dear light movers, the more highly evolved you become, the more challenges arise to help you grow. Remember, even the dark serves the light, and it is up to you to continually move light into darkness *every time you find it.* You are here to move light into the third dimension and bring multidimensional consciousness Home to Earth.

Chapter Four

FOUNDATION

*"Can you imagine a new core
basis to support you beyond your
planetary foundation of earth,
air, fire, and water?"*

The Elements of Foundation

We would be pleased to give you more depth and scope of understanding of your physical world and your place in it. We wish to expand your understanding in order to help you move beyond your third- dimensional perceptions of what creates reality by examining the foundation of reality. All foundations carry the energy of four; humans currently define the physical realm through the four elements of earth, air, fire, and water. We will help you to understand how these elements relate to *you*, and then we will share with you our perspective of the foundation of the true reality. Everything comes from energy, and physical elements are no different. They bring the consciousness of the energy from which they are made, just as you carry the consciousness of your energy. The consciousness of each element contributes to *your* consciousness.

Water

You are water beings on a water planet. Most of this planet is made of water, and *you* are made of water. Most of what you are in the physical is expressed in liquid, moveable, fluid form. You are wave motion, even though you think of yourselves as being solid. You wave in and out of various aspects of being. Water manifests in three structures on this planet: solid as ice, liquid as flowing water, and gas as steam, or the mist that forms when water condenses into air. You yourselves are comprised of three distinct forms of water. You may compare your bones to solid water, like ice. Your blood is like liquid water. You breathe water in and out in the air as gas. (As you know, air contains water.) It is through water that you communicate; it is water that carries the message. This is why it is so deeply important to monitor the thoughts that you think, for each thought goes into the collective water of humanity in order to manifest the reality of your lives. Each thought ripples through the water of humanity, affecting the condition of the sea of your collective consciousness. We have discussed this in great detail in *Conversations With Laarkmaa*. It would be wise to learn to take responsibility for every thought, if you wish to clean up the collective waters of humanity and the waters of Earth, thereby stopping war, having better relationships, and healing yourselves and the planet.

You may also compare your belief systems to varying forms of water. For example, your more rigidly held beliefs are like ice: hard, dense, and immovable. Other beliefs are more fluid and changeable, like liquid water. As you begin to release firmly held beliefs, you allow more flow into your energy field and realm of possibilities, representing the more expansive and gaseous state of water. Your thoughts become as light and airy as gas. As each belief becomes more and more fluid, you will eventually be able to release them all. Your thoughts are like water in the form of gas, or waves of etheric energy that move into space.

One of the greatest things that you can do to heal yourselves is to understand and work with water. We have suggested that you release the belief that you are only solid beings in physical forms. You are not. You are fluid; you are wave motion; you are moving energy. If you wish to heal the human condition, you need to better understand yourselves as water. You have forgotten that you are shape-shifters who can move in and out of energetic form at any time according to how you choose to energize yourselves and manifest your energy. If you pay attention to water, such as watching a stream flow, you will see that water always knows how to move around or over obstacles. If you watch when substances are placed into water, you will also see that water knows how to absorb or dissolve things. Water can move anything into a different state or location. Remember that your physical body is made of salt water, just like the waters of the planet, so you, too, can move around or over obstacles. You, too, can absorb, dissolve, or change energy.

We speak to you more about water than any other element because it is so instrumental to your understanding Who You Are as waves of energy. Looking more closely at water can help you to understand your fluid makeup and better connect you to your environment and to each other. Remember that the only constant in the third dimension is change, and water reminds you of how changeable you can be. When you communicate water-to-water with others, you can communicate everything about Who You Are. (We have spoken about this in more detail in *Conversations With Laarkmaa.*) Once you recognize and understand how you connect and communicate through water, you may also learn how to transport yourself through water—and we don't mean on a boat. Water is indeed magic!

Air

Understanding the various components that make up the element air in the third dimension will help you to understand how air supports life. Externally you experience the movement of air as wind. Internally you experience the movement of air as breathing. Air represents movement and space. External air, or wind, creates movement and space on Earth. Air carries seeds to pollinate the plant kingdom and moves clouds so that they can deliver rain where it is needed. Air moves stagnant energy and brings fresh energy into your environment.

Air *always* represents movement and the constancy of change. Nowhere is this more apparent than in the movement of your own breath, where your body takes in oxygen to support life, and then processes carbon dioxide to regulate your entire physical system. You breathe continually throughout each moment of your life on Earth, and your breathing is one very important function that keeps you in harmony with the rhythms of Earth. There is also a still point in your breathing to allow your body to process the air you have taken in before you release it. From the space of each still point, movement begins again, allowing you to constantly and continually flow with the movement of life.

One thing that will support your evolution is to allow space for movement to occur. If you fill all your space with busy thoughts, unresolved emotions, and habitual actions, there is no space for you to remember what is real. You have *filled* your current space with third-dimensional illusions and attachments to beliefs. Allow air to help you to change this. Begin to notice the space in your breathing and to create space for new ways to experience life. Air can help you understand how to approach all of your interactions with less density and to live more lightly on Earth.

Fire

The element of fire is one of the foundational elements on Earth because it provides heat and light to support life. You use fire to warm yourselves and to cook your food. At a more basic level, your sun, which is fire, warms the entire planet and offers nutrition to the plants and other living beings on Earth, including you. Fire is light, and through a more thorough understanding of fire, you may begin to understand how the light that you *are* is vital to the evolutionary process of life on Earth.

Please remember that we have often referred to *you* as divine sparks of light. You connect Source to Who You Are through the energy of light. You are, in fact, here to bring your light into the world of form. This perception can help you to understand the element of fire and how it relates to you. Fire is the most important element for the transmutational process of change. On a physical level, fire will burn anything that needs to be destroyed to make room for new growth. In *you*, the energy of fire can help you to burn or transcend anything that is in the way of your growth. Fire can light your way through any place of chaos that arises from ungoverned thoughts. Yet the light of fire must be used consciously, both in the physical world and in your own conscious evolution. The divine spark of Who You Are is controlled and directed by your will and needs to be regulated in the process of transformation; fire that is not controlled can and will burn up anything in its way.

We have heard humans say, "You burn me up!" when they are angry. The choice of those words comes from a place deep within your consciousness where you are aware that fire can help you transcend the emotional feelings that are "burning you up." People who have "fiery tempers" often believe that they are expressing their emotions or what they think they need to correct in others; they have a misguided perception of *who* it is that needs to transform. Of course, the one experiencing the "burning emotion" is always the one responsible for changing. Positive transformation requires the use of your fire and your will to examine your thoughts and reconnect them to your heart. Let the fire light your way to use your will, so that you neither "flare up" in anger nor suppress what needs to be said (which can cause a buildup of pressure in your emotional field that will likely erupt, like the pressure inside a volcano on Earth).

Fire is the element most closely associated with the process of ascension. You can see that as you look at the physical effects of fire on Earth. The planet is releasing more and more fire from Her internal core now because Earth is preparing to transmute, transcend, and ascend into a different form. She is changing. As light movers, you who are sensitive and aware are experiencing the effects of many of these changes in your physical bodies, causing you some discomfort as you adjust. The light of fire illuminates the merging of your light bodies and your physical bodies together. Pay attention to physical fire in your third-dimensional world, and begin to see the fire, or light, within you as divine light beings.

Earth

You already know that the element of earth consists of the soil (or dirt) that covers the planet everywhere that there is no water. This soil provides a support and foundation for living plants and trees to grow. Of course, Earth is comprised of the other elements we have already discussed, as well as the earth element. An even deeper understanding of your relationship to Earth tells you that you are *part* of Her. You are the neurological system of Earth. The energy you express through your experiences affects Earth directly through Her neurological system: *you*. You are electromagnetic beings who send an energetic charge into your atmosphere through every single energy that you express: through thought, word, and deed. Collectively, for all humans are connected, this is the energy that runs through the Earth as Her neurological system. Just as your neurons govern the expression of your movements, Earth expresses movement through earthquakes, weather patterns, volcanic activity, and other forms of Earth changes. All of these movements affect the earth element. Additionally, the collective of humanity, which makes up most of the unconscious members of society worldwide, views the earth only as a collection of resources to be thoughtlessly taken and used. As conscious light movers, you understand that Earth is more just than a group of elements to be used for human consumption, and that if you undermine the foundation of the planet, you will disrupt the harmonic balance necessary for life on Earth. You need to bring more awareness of this dynamic relationship into the collective.

Earth is more than the single earth element, and you are much more than the elemental aspects of Earth. Earth herself represents the more dense physical elements of the third dimension. She is in the process of ascension, moving out of the constrictions of dense physical form into a lighter expression of energy through the process of ascension in consciousness, just as you are. Your choices affect that process, as Her process affects you. Begin to notice how the earth supports you and be supportive of Her through the choices you make individually and together.

A New Foundation

The world that you experience is much larger than you imagine. Much of your understanding of the third-dimensional physical aspects of your experience on Earth is based on your concept that the world is comprised of four *physical* elements: earth, air, fire, and water. These elements are real and *do* comprise your *physical* reality, yet there is a larger, more universal reality that is built upon a more multidimensional understanding of elements. We would like to enhance your understanding of this reality by showing you how the four aspects of love, trust, joy, and compassion create a foundation that both includes your current understanding and expands *beyond* what you perceive and experience here in the third dimension. You can begin to build a better world through building upon this new foundation.

Increasing your understanding of how love, trust, joy, and compassion create a foundation for life will raise your consciousness, and as this occurs, your vibration will also be raised, enhancing *how* you express in physical form. As you integrate a higher understanding of what makes a true foundation, you will begin to expand how you express yourselves through your heart energy, your wave motion, your spark of light, your moving breath, and your ability to show compassion for all. The foundation of love, trust, joy, and compassion is based on universal truth and will support your essence more than a simple, physical foundation that is based only on the elements of water, air, fire, and earth. You will discover the power of this larger, universal foundation as you wake up and begin to heal the human condition.

To expand your understanding of third-dimensional reality into the larger universal reality, begin to broaden your thoughts about each physical element on Earth and how it relates to the universal elements we describe. For example, you can think about how you and the planet are both made of water, and how water is the element that allows communication heart to heart. Broaden your thinking to think of water, which is the basis of all life on Earth, as being equivalent to love, the basis of *everything* in the universe. You have just expanded your understanding of the first and most foundational element of life. Life on Earth is based on water. Universal life is based on love.

Now do the same thing as you think about air, which supports life on Earth. Notice your breath. Notice how naturally you breathe air in and out without having to think about it. You simply *trust* that your body knows how to breathe air and always will. Now broaden your thinking. Air supports life on Earth, and *trust* is the support for love. Love requires trust, both on Earth and universally. Perhaps you can see now how and why *trust* is an essential foundational element of universal reality.

Fire (or light) on Earth is part of your physical foundation because you require light and fire to warm you, grow your food, and nourish you. The universal equivalent to light and fire is *joy*. As a universal foundational element, joy supports your ability to trust and to love. Conversely, when you feel joyful, you are more easily able to trust in the universe and to love each other. When you allow yourselves to experience full connection with one another, you experience joy. So please broaden your understanding of the physical aspect of fire, or light, to the more expansive understanding of joy as a universal foundational element.

The physical element of earth is the last physical foundational element we wish to help you understand from a larger perspective. Your planet, Earth, is named after the physical element of earth. You may begin to expand your understanding of the foundation the earth element provides by thinking about how you are cared for by the planet. Earth exhibits great compassion for all of Her creatures. *You* are here experiencing the extreme density of physical form, through which you are learning to apply more compassion to everything and everyone on Earth. If you understand Earth as a living, compassionate being and yourselves as part of Earth, then it becomes easy to see that the final foundational aspect of the universal foundation is compassion, which is equivalent to earth.

The elements of your third-dimensional world—water, air, fire, and earth—are stronger and more potent than anything that exists in the third-dimension alone, for these energies make up everything that is *real* here on Earth. Yet the universal foundation of love, trust, joy, and compassion is the *real* foundation that will support your evolution into multidimensional beings. Being in physical form, yet *simultaneously remembering* the other aspects of Who You Are, gives you a powerful and perfect staging ground from which to do your work. You chose to come to Earth, whether you remember that choice or not, to help humanity evolve. The most essential element to use to support your work is the foundational element of compassion. As you exercise compassion with everyone and everything around you, accepting and integrating all parts into the whole, the other essential elements of universal foundation can move into place to create a basis for an expanded and multidimensional reality here on Earth. Compassion supports your feelings of joy; joy supports your ability to trust; trust supports your complete and total ability to love.

This book contains energy and words to remind you of what your hearts remember. We have placed seeds of awakening in your energetic field through the words we have shared. Assimilating what we are sharing and beginning to live from the foundation we are suggesting contributes to the evolution of your consciousness and to the healing of the human condition.

Manifestation

When you understand and practice what we have suggested to utilize the principles of a universal foundation, rather than simply focusing on a third-dimensional physical foundation, you will be able to manifest a more harmonious world. Humans are great manifestors; that is, you have the *potential* to co-creatively manifest a great world, but you do not yet understand how to do it. Currently you are manifesting chaos, confusion, separation, and pain through consistently sending out misguided thoughts and erroneous beliefs that you hold individually and collectively. We wish to help you correct your imbalanced manifestations and learn to manifest in harmony with universal truth and flow.

All of the principles of manifestation are directly connected to the expanded foundational elements we have just explained. To work with them, you must first recognize and take responsibility for your own emotions (the signposts that tell you that something is out of harmony). Secondly, you must control, contain, and direct your thoughts, your mental co-creative energy, through the use of your will. Direct *each* thought through the single, unified energy of love. Direct each thought to come from the divine spark of light that exists within the heart of each of you before you send it outwardly towards the world. Your current way of thinking releases scattered, emotional, and judgmental thoughts that coalesce to form a chaotic physical world. *It does not have to be so.* You make it much harder than is necessary. Living in a world of duality, you experience the highs and lows of circumstance, but you have not learned that your mental thoughts create your reality according to your *response to and relationship with* what you encounter.

The third principle for proper manifestation is constancy. To manifest healthy harmonious lives, you must be *constant* in turning your thoughts towards love and sending your light around each thought that you create. When you allow yourselves to believe that the duality you are experiencing is the only truth, you experience more contrast between light and dark, and between joy and suffering. When you are constant, using your will to serve your heart, light and dark begin to work together to serve your evolution. It is possible to feel the joy of a pain that tells you something is out of harmony, rather than becoming a victim to the suffering.

Although you have forgotten how to use your power to *positively* manifest, we are reminding you that you are able to co-create through constantly choosing to return to your instinctual awareness, allowing it to pull you closer and closer into harmony with the universe through love. We remind you to choose to follow the instinct for love in each given moment, rather than responding to survival instincts that you have been incorrectly taught and that only take you further into separation. You will not be safe following concepts of "survival of the fittest," which are based on primitive responses to fear. *That will never keep you safe.* Humans have never been safe by following that kind of fear-based reaction to life. In the moments where the human heart expands through trust, declaring that you know you are safe regardless of what is going on in the environ-ment, the energy around you shifts and changes. Many stories are told about such energetic shifts that support and enhance your survival. You call them miracles. We call them the natural order of events, when you are responding through your true instinct. For example, the story of a mother being able to effort-lessly lift an entire automobile off of her trapped child clearly demonstrates the power of an instinctive response based on love. Responding to life through love, not fear, will always keep you safe. To meet challenges in this way, simply remember that you can only be safe in love, for love is the highest power; in unity, it is the *only* power.

As long as you allow yourselves to descend into the energy of lower-vibrational responses, you will continue to create the same repetitious patterns that you are experiencing now. Fight, humans! This is a battle that moves you toward the ultimate separation or the truth of unity. Love everything that comes to you and use it for your own growth. This how light meets dark and how the beautiful rainbow of all that you are begins to form. This is how you command the dark to serve the light and move evolution towards the unity of love. If humanity can summon the will and the courage to be constant in your thoughts of light, you will begin to manifest a physical reality of light and love. We love you.

Chapter Five

TOOLS FOR CHANGE

*"Once you begin new patterns
of thought and behavior, change
is inevitable."*

Overview

W̶e offer the following exercises to help you break patterns that no longer serve you. We provide these exercises in the middle of the book so that you may begin to integrate the changes we are suggesting as you read. Of course, you may choose to engage in these exercises or not, at any time, according to your own particular needs and interest. We do hope you enjoy them. Use them as your heart directs. We love you greatly.

Restoring Emotional Balance

If you are emotionally upset or experiencing physical distress, you can calm yourself through breathing in the foundational essences we described in the previous chapter. Slowly begin to breathe and concentrate your thoughts on each of these elements.

Breathe in love.
Breathe out trust.
Breathe in joy.
Breathe out compassion.

Do this repeatedly until you calm yourself and return to balance. Remember to include gratitude in this practice as well, finding things in your life for which you are grateful. Be grateful for your own gifts and talents, for the people and animals you love, for the beauty of Nature all around you, and for anything that makes you happy. Being grateful helps to adjust your energy. As you feel the gratitude, remember these things:

You are not alone. Help and support are always available. By calming yourself through this exercise, you are more easily able to listen to the help that is always here. By this, we mean that as you calm down and begin to rebalance yourself, your vibration is raised to meet the energies of those around you who wish to help (your guides, angels, spirit helpers, and interdimensional beings like us).

Using Colors to Balance Emotions

Emotions are both the biggest stumbling block for humanity, as well as humanity's greatest promise for release from dysfunctional patterns of behavior. Emotions may be managed and utilized for change through proper understanding of their function. Here is an exercise to help you. Use your imagination to visualize these colors until you learn to actually see the colors or feel the energy of their presence.

Begin by imagining a column of emerald green light pouring into the crown of your head. Emerald green energy is a creative and healing energy that enhances your vitality and can also help rebalance your emotions. Visualize this energy moving down from your crown chakra all the way to your feet and then back up again. Now invite in energy of the color violet, which can be used for transformation. See it as a beautiful violet cloud of stardust over your head. Move your emotions towards the violet light. When you are feeling heartsick or heavy, you may use the combination of moving green energy through you, and then releasing your emotions to the cloud of beautiful violet light. Use this as a meditative practice whenever you are experiencing emotional discomfort or pain. It is a wonderful exercise that can help you immensely.

Here is another color exercise you may use for emotional equilibrium. Enjoy it! Begin to visualize pink light flowing into your heart; allow that energy to move from your heart throughout your entire body. Now visualize the pink energy spreading from you out into the world. Once you feel the pink energy completely filling and surrounding you, invite a flow of white light into your crown. Feel the stream of white light pouring into you. Now see the white light move down from your crown until it begins to radiate and swirl around your entire being. The white light will help you remove the illusions that you have carried throughout your life, and the pink light will restore your heart to its natural feeling state of love. You will feel lighter when you are finished.

Working with Pain

Pain is a form of imbalance or discomfort that signals that you not in harmony with rhythms of life and universal energies. When you are in discomfort or experiencing pain, you are experiencing a state of dis-ease. Become quiet in order to allow your mind to reach the place where you can *actually* understand where the pain or discomfort originates or to what it is related. Only by quieting yourselves to the degree that you shut out as much outer sensation and stimuli as possible, will you reach this place of connecting with the original source of the dis-comfort and how it can teach you to resolve the issue. Quiet your mind. Relax your body. Listen to your breathing and your heartbeat. Listen deeply in the quiet. Joining the rhythms of your breath, the earth, and the universe will help you to find what is out of balance.

Focus on the point within you that is causing the most distress or that represents the most dis-ease. First accept the pain; you must always accept an energy as it *is* before you can work to change it. Visualize yourself compressing that energy into the smallest point you can imagine. Once the pain has been compressed into a small point, you will be ready to move it. Invite a golden stream of light, representing grace, into your physical body through your head, your heart, or your solar plexus. Once the golden light is flowing through you, move the compressed pain into the stream of that golden light. Imagine the golden light clearing and cleansing this point of pain.

Increasing Your Will Power

Much of the discord you experience in your lives comes because you have not focused your will to keep your thoughts flowing in a harmonious, positive direction. This exercise will assist you in stopping old patterns of discord and nurturing new patterns of positive response to life circumstances.

When you first notice that something does not feel joyful or harmonious (whether with another person or in a situation), *notice* what you are feeling. Usually you feel that something does not match *your* flow, and you do not *like* what is occurring. *Notice* first what you are feeling. *Notice* second the thoughts that you are thinking connected to what is occurring. Usually you *think* that someone has overridden or disregarded what is important to you, or you *think* that the weather is not what you want, or you *think* that what someone has done is inappropriate, or you *think* some other thought of discord about what is out of resonance with what *you* want.

Now *define* what you are feeling: anger, frustration, grief, jealousy, fear, etc. The emotion surfaces to show you how you yourself are out of balance.

Now *breathe* in and out. *Stop* thinking about what you are feeling and just breathe. *Stop* blaming and judging others or situations for being or doing something other than what *you* want. Simply *breathe* in and out, using your will to focus on your breath only. Imagine you can see the light that comes in to you through your will center. That light is your connection to Source. Now you can begin thinking again by *using your will* to redirect your thoughts into a more positive and harmonious state.

Invite in *gratitude* for anything that broadens and deepens your own perspective. *Stop thinking* about what you have judged and *be thankful* for the new perspective. *Free* yourself from needing to be in control of your own situation, and become more accepting of what you have *perceived* to be out of harmony with your desires. *Free yourself* from needing to be in control. As you use your will to redirect your thoughts into a more positive and harmonious space, you will notice that the emotion begins to transform into a higher feeling state.

In summary:

1 ~ Notice what you feel.

2 ~ Look at the thoughts you connect with the emotion.

3 ~ Define the emotion that is showing you how you are out of balance.

4 ~ Stop thinking, judging, and blaming.

5 ~ Breathe in and out, using your will center to redirect your thoughts to a more positive polarity.

6 ~ Be grateful for new perspectives.

7 ~ Free yourself from needing to be in control.

8 ~ Notice that your feelings have come back into harmony.

This process will take your thoughts from your will center to your heart, and as your heart expands with love and light, your thoughts will spin off into the universe as a gift, an essence of positive energy. Automatically when you do this, you will notice that your feeling state also changes. Your emotions will subside because you regain harmony within your own essence. Your feeling state is now raised in vibration and you can begin to co-create a higher vibratory state in your environment, allowing love and light to fill you and all others for a manifestation of harmonious unity. We trust that this exercise of utilizing your will may assist you in clearing out old patterns where you feel

REMEMBERING WHO WE ARE

disregarded, overridden, disrespected, or out of harmony. Those old patterns will fall away as you do this exercise regularly.

The Importance of Laughter

Laughter is one of the most important tools you can use to change your perception and alter your mood. We have spoken to you often about using humor or laughter to change the severity of a reaction to anything that you either do not like or do not approve of as it comes into your environment. We do not mean laughing at the expense of others; we mean genuine joy-filled laughter that can be shared by all. Even if you yourself cannot change something, you can always laugh at what and how it arrives in your life. Laughter will always illuminate any situation that seems challenging or even absurd. You cannot be outraged, upset, or dismayed by anything if you are laughing at what is happening. Learn to laugh at any occurrence you believe is disrupting or challenging your life, rather than adversely reacting through anger, disappointment, or grief. As you laugh, you will notice that not only does your mood improve, but your physical sensations of stress and tension dissipate as well. Change is a constant in life. Learn to use laughter in combination with all the many changes you encounter, and you will flow through them more easily. When things seem not to be working in your life, just laugh at the circumstances, and that act will help to lighten any situation. Using humor can always be uplifting and help return you to a state of joy.

Asking and Receiving

It is important to ask for help when you need it. There are many beings of light waiting to give you the help that you request. The more you take responsibility for your fifty percent to change, the more easily they can help you. Ask for all aspects of yourself to be filled with the white light of truth so that you can easily release your illusions. Ask for the golden light of grace to remove the effects of all karma. Ask to be filled with the green healing light to correct any imbalances in your system. Ask to be surrounded by the blue light of trust to enhance your ability to trust in each other and the universe. Ask for the violet light to transform everything in you and around you that does not support unity. Ask to be illumined by the yellow light and to experience joy. Ask to be filled with the pink light of love to expand your ability to *be* love and to give love. Give thanks to all those who help you.

Laarkmaa's Heart Meditation

We would like to invite you to help us, if you choose, to restore the Heart of Humanity through an exercise with color. We would like to remind you as we work with this, what the energy vibrations of each color resonate with and how you may utilize that energy. We will lead you through the exercise and ask you to visualize what you can. You are going to begin with recognizing the energy of the heart; the energy of the heart needs to be placed back into humanity. It has been suppressed and ignored for too long. It is time that the power of love, the energy of the heart, reach its rightful place to lead humanity.

So begin in any way you choose by seeing the pink light of love in a ball of energy in front of you. Feel that ball of pink light in front of you. That is the love from your heart, and that is the love from the universe, and it is yours. As you recognize it, and as you feel the energy of that pink light of love, you can begin to feel tingles through your body. You can feel a resonance with love energy. Remember, with love energy, no fear can exist. See the pink light of love emanating all around, as if you hold it in your hands in front of you. See it moving into your heart and back from your heart, and see it moving out across the planet and across the heavens. See it going into the heart of every human being on the planet. Take a moment to breathe in the pink light of love and breathe it out, sending it to the heart of each human on Earth.

Tone briefly using the vibratory sound that opens the heart…. Ahhhhhhh. We will tone with you while you are holding this ball of pink energetic love light. Use the tones to help carry the love and light you are sending into the heart of every human on earth. Ahhhhhhhh……

Now *feel* that energy vibrating through you, and know that you are loved and that you *are* love. As you focus, softly gazing at the pink light, notice that there is a blue light surrounding the pink. It is the energetic vibration of trust, for trust is built upon love. See that soft blue light radiating around the ball of energy you are holding in your hand: pink in the center, blue around it. Feel the energy of trust permeating every cell of your being. You feel calm. You feel peaceful. That is the energy of trust. And as you feel that in yourself, look for us. We always represent ourselves as blue waves so that you can trust that we bring you truth. Our energy carries the energy of trust along with the energy of love. See that blue wavy energy around the pink ball that you hold, and then begin to send those blue waves out across the planet to each human heart that is filled with the pink light of love. Surround that energy now with the blue light of trust so that they may feel what it is like to be safe, to be calm, to trust. Take a few moments and send that to all of your brothers and sisters across the planet, and send it into your own heart as well: the blue energy of trust.

Now look and you will see the golden light of grace radiating down from the heavens, from the universe, into the ball that you are holding in front of you: pink love light in the center, trust around it, and golden light of grace beginning to radiate so that you see waves of gold surrounding the blue. This is the energy that releases all karma. This is the energy of grace. This is the energy that Christ Consciousness taught and Mary Magdalene taught, that when you have love and trust, grace can erase everything. Allow the golden light of grace to enter into your own heart. Feel it, knowing that you have choice to take responsibility with the energy of grace for what comes next. Send the golden light of grace to each human heart across the planet, freeing all from the binding ties of karma, allowing the grace to remove them from the pain and suffering so that they may begin to understand *how* to be different. Send the golden light of grace into each heart. It shimmers and vibrates. It is beautiful. Send it with love and trust: grace for all humanity.

Now see the green healing light: beautiful, brilliant, emerald green. It is all around the waves of gold, so that you have pink in the center, surrounded by blue, surrounded by gold, and now there is green. Now that you have the energy of love, trust, and grace, you can begin to heal. So heal yourselves, Dear Ones. Invite in the healing energy to heal every split between you and other, every split between heart and mind, every split between right and wrong, every split between "my way" and "your way." Allow the green energy to radiate healing until there is no more separation. There is only unity. And unity is big enough to hold all aspects so that each human being can follow her or his path without conflict, using love, trust, and grace. Now send that green healing light from yourself forward into all humans across the planet. Send it with the intention that it heal all splits: All splits of my country-your country. All splits of my oil-your oil, my money-your money. All splits between "I am right" and "you are wrong." All splits between my God and your God. All splits between brain and heart. All splits between you and me. Send that green healing energy out to all humanity. Send your intention on your breath.

With love, trust, and grace, may each human being heal. Now, Dear Ones, notice a brilliant yellow light shining down on you. Notice also the same light, brilliant yellow, is coming out of your own heart, for it is your divine spark, and it is connected with the light of illumination of the universe. Illumination—this is part of what the Christ Consciousness was bringing to humanity, the illumination to see the truth. Look at the yellow light. It is brilliant and it illuminates your way so that you can see how to be fully present in each present moment, listening, looking, and taking responsibility for everything you think, everything you feel, and everything you do, so that it resonates in unity for the highest good of all. Feel the golden light of grace reaching out and touching the green light of healing and then touching the yellow light of illumination. They are connected. When you heal because you have accepted grace, you can become illuminated, and when you are illuminated, you can see the truth. Send that beautiful yellow light forward into each human heart, so that each human heart may experience the love, the trust, the grace, the healing, and the illumination. See that light reaching each human heart, from your heart to theirs and from the universe into each of you, helping you to awaken to Who You Are, the new beings, the new humanity.

Now, Dear Ones, notice the brilliant white Christ light, the light of truth shining into your heart, surrounding, radiating all around this ball of energy you are holding in front of you; the white light of truth that you have reached by moving from love to trust to grace to illumination to truth, with healing. Notice it is *all* there *all* around you, and send forth into the heart of every human being the white light of truth, so that they may dispel all of their belief systems and all of their patterns of behavior, moving instead into the foundation that all beings are one; you are divine beings of love who have the capacity to trust one another, to be compassionate with one another, to support one another with love. Send forth the white light of truth so that all may awaken, if they choose.

Now, Dear Ones, we approach the final color. It is the violet light of transformation. See it radiating around the ball of energy you hold in front of you. It is waving all around. It is the energy of transformation. It is the energy of transmutation. With this energy, you can change anything. This is the energy of *change*. See it all around you. Send forth into each human heart across the planet the ability to change, the ability to transcend their beliefs, the ability to transmute old patterns of behavior and to be different. Send the violet light to each human heart so that they may experience it.

Now, notice if you will, that you have a radiating ball of seven colors in front of you. It is a torus *(a spiraling geometric pattern)*. It is the energy of the human heart. It is time, Dear light movers, that you take this energy, and you place it back in its rightful place for the heart of humanity. As you send this torus of energy out to each human heart on the planet, you are awakening the heart of all, and you are sending the energy back where it belongs. Send this torus with love and trust...the pink light of love, the blue light of trust, the golden light of grace, the green light of healing, the yellow light of illumination, the white light of truth, the violet light of transformation. Send it forth, and as you send it, you will see sparks of light all across the planet. These are the light movers who are connecting with you through silver threads of connecting light, weaving a web, a net to hold you, as you create the form of a new humanity.

We love you. Remember this exercise, for it is helping to awaken Who You Are, and use it to bring peace to your world.

(You will also find this meditation on Laarkmaa's Youtube channel at www.youtube.com/watch?v=N6Xc33ZdSdw).

Chapter Six

PURPOSE

*"Your purpose is to bring a higher
level of consciousness to the planet,
and to heal all separation."*

Life Purpose

Many of you have asked, "What is my purpose in life?" Your work here is to heal the heart of humanity and to reintegrate your hearts and minds together, so that your hearts direct you towards truth, and your minds can act through your heart's guidance. We will speak of your purpose from varying angles now. You have such a great choice in front of you. The first choice is to continue to dwell in the shadows and patterns that you are accustomed to within the limits of third-dimensional reality. The other choice is to transcend all of the dysfunctional beliefs that keep you in illusion in your current experience on Earth, and through this transcendence, create a peaceful world. *You have two distinct choices.* In the first reality, you experience life as frightened, competitive beings who are blocked in your growth through attachment to dysfunctional beliefs. The second reality is achieved when you choose to take responsibility for your thoughts and actions and to honor the painful emotions that propel you towards change. Make that choice, and you will then become the co-creators you are designed to be.

You already know what your purpose is; we have alluded to it many times in this book. Your purpose here is to awaken to the truth of multidimensional reality by raising your consciousness and shedding the deep patterns of blame, judgment, competition, and everything that causes separation. Your purpose is to begin to live in harmony. Many of you *think* that you need to be healers, counselors, or teachers. We tell you, the time for teachers, leaders, and healers is over, because *each* human has these abilities within them. Placing yourself in a special position as a "teacher" or "healer" is a continuation of hierarchical separation. Learn to see that these abilities are available to *all* who take responsibility to awaken to their true potential.

Your purpose is not about *what* you chose to do; it is about *how* you choose to do it. It does not matter what you choose to do; you will be just as effective in anything you choose to do, as long as you follow the precepts we have outlined for you. You will start to feel your purpose fulfilled when you recognize the gifts each of you have, and you begin to cooperate with one another in transparency. As you take responsibility to shift your own conscious awareness and the way you respond to life, your higher vibrations will affect everyone else. Change will be inevitable.

When you think of your life's purpose, begin to examine how your choices can affect all of humanity. Begin to release expectations, judgments, fears, and beliefs, all of which lie on the human side of the Veil of Illusion that you have created. We know some of you are beginning to see, hear, sense, and understand things differently, and that you are willing to move beyond the Veil of Illusion. The Veil of Illusion keeps you stuck in a state of confusion and density. Stretching beyond the veil by moving beyond patterned thoughts and belief systems will help humanity move to a higher vibratory state. You need to stop believing that your dense physical reality is the *only* truth that exists. *You are so much more than that.* You have the ability to move beyond the restrictions of the third dimension into the light beings that you are. Be in positive relationship with the universe, with Earth, with each other, and within yourselves. Be in relationship with love. Be in love. *Be* love. Because it feels wonderful to give, giving love is healing to all. This is the way to heal the human condition, and *this is your purpose.* By the time this book is in print, you will certainly have an escalated sense of greater potentials and possibilities, *if* you are paying attention and doing your work.

We remind you again here that your emotions are a gift. They are here to guide you towards fulfilling your purpose to live in harmony and love. Emotions scream at you to get your attention in order to tell you how you are out of balance. The more pain you feel, the more work you have to do. Whether you are feeling physical, mental, or emotional pain, you are feeling the press of the third dimension, and your purpose is to transcend it. Follow your emotions and your thoughts to see what is out of balance within yourselves, as we have guided you. Your work is to love what is in front of you, whatever it may be. When you feel pain, remember that you are focusing only on the third-dimensional aspect of reality. Use the pain to guide you and as your fuel for change. Pain is *always* a signal that something in your perspective needs to shift. As you change your perspective, you alchemically begin to co-create a different reality. Shifting your perspective can only be achieved moment by moment. You are so deeply ingrained with what you have been taught and what you believe to be true, that it takes continual and constant work to move away from old familiar patterns and into the truth that you are beings of love and light, here to offer love to others and to yourselves. This is the most important thing you need to understand about your purpose. You are here simply to be love, to heal your separation, and to trust that anything is possible and abundantly available!

The separation you experience may be seen as a path towards unity if you understand why separation takes place. Separation exists in order for you to transcend it; when you learn to look and resonate with similarities rather than focusing on differences, you may move beyond the pain of separation. We know that this is quite a mysterious understanding to navigate. We also know that because waves of energy are arriving to raise your consciousness, by the time we place our energy in these words and you read them, the consciousness will be in place for you to take a breath and say, "Ah, I resonate with that; that makes sense." Although the waves of energy are here now to support you and raise your consciousness, you will only be able to understand higher truth if you have had the courage and used your will to do your work. Love your pain and love each other, as the duality of separation reaches its zenith.

Separation is something to be *transcended*, not something to be *endured*. Your awareness and understanding of separation is increasing, and your feelings of conflict are increasing in order to give you the opportunity to transcend separation. That is your purpose. Transcend separation, and you reach the state of harmony and love. The universe is giving you the gift and the opportunity for transcendence now. This is what you must achieve; this is your divine right and what you came here to do. Those of you who are light movers have the *added* purpose of moving others towards transcendence by demonstrating the power of love. We repeat, it is not about *what* you do; it is about *how* you do it. Step beyond your belief systems, move beyond your pain, and choose another path. Move with your hearts, focusing on love. If you feel trapped through experiencing so much dis-ease or pain, focus on loving yourself. Do nothing else until you return to balance. Just breathe in love and breathe out love. Breathe in love and breathe out love until you begin to feel a sense of healing, for that very action will attract the energy that you need most. When you feel a bit stronger and more balanced, you may practice doing that with others, too.

There will be ups and downs as you experience the waves of duality leading you to transcend separation. Do not doubt that, Dear Ones; each one of you has a spark of light to use for transcendence, no matter how much you feel it is covered or obscured, or that you cannot reach it. *It is there.* We see it, and as we see it from our perspective, you light up the planet. Even when it is behind your Veil of Illusion, we see the spark that is there from the light within your hearts. *It is there*; trust that this is real. Never give up trusting Who You *know* You truly Are.

Remember that as light movers, you volunteered to do this work; you chose to participate in raising the consciousness of humanity. This is your purpose. Humans who do not choose to participate will continue to feel separation and dis-ease; that is the path they choose. Yet if you choose to do as we suggest and make the move with the energies that are being offered, you will experience the greatest opportunity that humanity has ever known. Even though the great teachers like Christ, Mary Magdalene, Mohammed, and Buddha, were here to teach you how to fulfill your purpose, you have never been given as great an opportunity as you are being given now to recognize your own divinity and to fulfill your individual and collective purpose. This is your opportunity to turn continually towards love, even loving pain so that it dissolves around you. Recognize that some pain is necessary to take you where you are going. Allow yourselves to trust in the goodness of the universe. You have the power within you to transcend anything in order to fulfill your purpose. It would be very sad for you not to take the steps that are available to help you remember Who You Are. Shake off what is oppressing you. Shake off your disillusionment, your disenchantment, your broken hearts, your expectations, and even your hopes; shake off all of that and simply be in love.

You have chosen to come to Earth to serve by bringing a higher level of consciousness to the planet, and to heal all separation. As you come closer to fulfilling your purpose, you will be challenged by more intense experiences. You are experiencing many little deaths of relationships, financial structures, old styles of communication, and everything that needs to be transformed. You may relate these little deaths to the ancient Indian concept where the goddess Kali destroys everything that needs to end in order to create a new space for what is to come. You can no longer rely upon things to which you have been accustomed. As new energies are arriving on Earth, things simply will not work in the same way. Many of you are quite concerned with a lack of abundance as old structures (your homes, your jobs, and your finances) begin to fall apart. Please remember that old systems must be destroyed before new and better ones can come into place. Part of your purpose is to meet these challenges with love and trust, along with gratitude both for what you have and for what you are about to receive. Every time you feel that the third-dimensional world takes something from you or a wave of duality negatively affects you, be resilient and trust in the process.

The collective unconscious of humanity is unaware of the work that needs to be done. In fact, most of the collective are unaware of *anything* beyond their limited perspectives of third-dimensional reality. They are still very much focused on their beliefs in the dualistic extremes of right-wrong, good-bad, you-me, and judgment-based ideas that keep humanity separate and alone. You, as light movers, are coming to a place of pivotal understanding where everything that is superfluous to truth will be ripped away, giving you the opportunity to see the truth of the new reality and what is actually happening all around you through your multidimensional hearts and eyes.

The great expansion now occurring includes fully awakening to the presence of the Christ Consciousness and the Divine Feminine within each of you. You are being guided to remember the divine wisdom that is in each of you. This, too, is part of your purpose. Remember, you are responsible for returning the heart to humanity by removing the Veil of Illusions made of time and fear. Viewing everything through this veil of polar opposites, you have allowed judgment and blame to rip humanity's heart in two. You have allowed duality to separate you through all of the polarities that you have experienced, including the separation of the left and right hemispheres of your brain. It is time to reunite your minds and your hearts for the healing of humanity. Let your hearts lead you into remembering your true selves as divine human beings. Your true purpose has nothing to do with your choice of career. Fulfillment happens when you realize that you have everything you need inside of you, and a sense of purpose occurs when you are sharing your gifts. Please remember, it doesn't matter *what* you choose to do, only *how* you choose to do it. Find your purpose by healing the splits that have separated you and return to harmony and love.

The Purpose of Relationship

To heal the human condition, you must understand the purpose of relationship. Relationship is a key concept in healing. On a planet based on duality, which Earth is, everything has polar extremes or polar opposites; the entire purpose of interacting between extremes is to learn how to be in relationship with *everything*. Indigenous Earth elders have long told you that everything is connected, yet we would like to give you a deeper level of this understanding so that you can transmute your dualistic perspectives. Relationship is an interplay of energies that contain elements of both oppositeness and similarity. Humans become dis-eased and out of balance through focusing on the differences of opposites, rather than either seeing similarities, or seeing how opposites can support and contribute to a greater whole. Your focus on opposites has caused much separation and distress to your psyches, emotional bodies, and mental bodies, and dis-ease within your physical bodies. This distress and dis-ease is directly linked with how you relate to everything. Understanding how your differences are connected brings duality into unity. All aspects of your distress and dis-ease can be easily adjusted and corrected when everything is put into a better perspective, which comes through looking at relationship.

Relationship is simply about relating. You are on a planet where the powerful element of choice teaches you how to relate. Relationship has to do with *everything*; it is not only how you relate to other humans. It is also how you relate to us, as you listen to *our* perspective. It is about how you relate to each viewpoint that you receive, and it is about the relationship of what you give back to the universe through your own awareness or unawareness. Relationship is about how you govern your thoughts and opinions, how you govern your emotions, how you communicate, how you use your voice tones, and how you use your physical bodies. Do you utilize all of these energies to create resonance? Will you learn to relate through your hearts? Your relationships with your own hearts and minds govern how you relate with others. Most of you are badly trained to relate only as your minds or your emotions direct you. We see that you do take some actions through the guidance of your hearts, but often if your minds tell you that you are not receiving what you want or expect, you close your hearts and allow your minds to mislead you.

In order to fully understand relationship, you must first realize that how you relate with others stems from the relationship you experience internally within yourself. What kind of relationship do you have with yourself? Do you accept all aspects of yourself unconditionally? Do you release dysfunctional beliefs and patterns of behavior? Do you take responsibility to grow and change? Do you release artificial expectations or views of yourself in order to love Who You *truly* Are? Improving your relationship with yourself extends into how you vibrate and relate to others. You are here to do the work of deciding whether to allow your emotions, belief systems, and mental chatter to derail the peaceful harmony that is your birthright, or to relate through choosing vibrations and tones that resonate with states of love. You improve relationships with all others when you resolve your relationship with yourself.

When you are imbalanced within yourself, you begin to become imbalanced in relating to others. For example, when you are not happy with yourself, you may become disgruntled at work, feeling that your work is not satisfying. Your dissatisfaction at work may then extend into how you relate to others at home. Issues of improper relating can be seen quite easily in families: in children whose parents do not recognize Who They Are or in parents who try to mold their children into something that will fulfill what is missing inside of themselves. These ways of relating persist throughout your lives until you decide to break the dysfunctional patterns and cycles. When you learn to see every part of any relationship as an aspect of yourself, you find the balance point of all relationships; this vision quickly brings relationships back into harmony.

It is up to you whether you choose to be in relationships that are uncomfortable, or whether you wish to be only in relationships that promote and engender love. We are not suggesting that anyone stay in *any* relationship that is abusive; we are suggesting that you take responsibility and examine your own belief systems about what causes you harm and pain. All humans seek love in relationships, whether it is a parent-child love, the deep interpersonal love of partnership, the love of friendship, or even the love of Earth. Love is what you seek. Sometimes your fears hide the truth of your search for love, and you focus on what you *hope* to receive, rather than simply loving what is before you. At other times, you are able to give love without expecting to receive anything in return, simply as a gift. *This* is unconditional love, and *this* is the basis of proper relating.

How you relate to Nature and the planet is also part of relationship. Do you simply take what you want from Earth without giving anything back? You are *part of* Nature, so everything you take without giving back takes something from yourselves as well. Simple respect dictates that you give back in exchange for what you receive. Learn to ask permission rather than simply assuming you can take what you want. This respect is necessary in *all* relationships.

We tell you, everything is connected through energetic relationship, and your relationships determine what your experiences will be. Everything consists of energy; energy is alive and has consciousness. We suggest that for a proper exchange in relating, you learn to respect and appreciate the exchange of energy with everyone and everything you meet. Learn how to relate to *everything* with proper energetic exchange. Ask yourselves in every situation, "Am I relating with respect and love?" Examine how you relate to the plant kingdom and to animals. Do you pick up, throw, or kick rocks as if they are lifeless? Do you cut down trees without their permission? Do you take from animals, assuming that you have the right to take their lives for your food? You have the choice to stop being in dualistic relationships where you always take from animals and animals are *forced* to give their lives or their byproducts.

How you engage in relationship applies to everything around you in the physical world. What is so special about living on Earth is that you have the ability to *choose* how to be in every relationship. We are asking you now to expand your focus, to move your energy away from thinking and believing that everything exists separately from yourselves. Expand your understanding of relationship so that you begin to *relate* to the consciousness of everything. Expand your awareness of how you relate in thoughts and actions. So many of your relationships are competitive and aggressive because of your belief systems that *you* are "right" and others are "wrong." Relationships can never be harmonious and balanced when you engage in such dualistic perceptions. Begin to appreciate how all varying aspects make up the whole, and learn how to relate to one another through respect and the proper exchange of energy.

Your financial structure is an excellent example of imbalanced relating. Until humanity understands the concept of proper energetic exchange and restructures your finances, you will continue to have imbalanced and dysfunctional relationships with money. Because of your emphasis on the importance of money, this imbalance influences *all* of your other relationships. You need to learn to give back to others in balanced proportion to what you receive in *every* relationship, whether it involves money or anything else. There can no longer be a focus on money as the only form of energetic exchange. What humanity needs to understand is that true and proper energetic exchange needs to be comprised of the exchanging of equal gifts rather than an exchange of an artificial representation called money. We have asked humans in varying places around the globe to stop charging money for what they do, and instead to enter into a practice of giving freely from your hearts and asking others to meet you by giving back in value for what they receive. Continuing to still use money as a temporary symbol of your appreciation for what you receive is a transitional act, but eventually you must evolve beyond the reliance on money and make a fair exchange of your gifts and talents.

Until you completely eliminate money, you can make exchanges by reaching an agreement together of the value that will be exchanged for services. When you decide on an exchange together, you are more likely to approach an energetic balance that supports the highest good of all. When you find relationships that honor proper energetic exchange, you will also find unconditional love. Proper exchange in *all* relationships leads to abundance for *all*, for when you give through unconditional love, you do not compete with one another; instead you begin to cooperate and share what is available for all. This form of exchange enhances true abundance in all relationships.

As the consciousness of duality comes to a close, the importance of balanced relating is increased. You may experience increasing conflicts in your relationships on Earth simply because differences that were masked before become more apparent in the new energies that you are experiencing. You may even feel larger and larger extremes of difference and conflict. Your job is to notice these differences in order to harmonize them. Everything that is opposite to anything else will show its potential for creating conflict or competition. These extremes of difference increase in order for you to harmonize them by transcending challenges and beginning to relate together. Begin to find similarities between you, rather focusing on your differences. Opposites are only seeing the same thing from a different vantage point, seeing a different flavor or texture of universal oneness. Everything is one. The purpose of the evolution of humanity is to transcend all conflict by recognizing that everything is connected; harmonizing differences can bring you closer together in unity.

You may sometimes need to alter your perceptions to promote more harmony within a relationship. The way you *feel* about what you see or experience has its own dynamic energy. Remember that emotions are only signposts to point the way to your true state of being. Each *emotion* you feel is the opposite of your true *feelings* of peace, joy, bliss, trust, and compassion. If you focus on the energy of imbalanced emotions, your relationships within yourselves and with others also become out of balance. Stay centered on the core of Who You truly Are as divine beings of love and light, and allow emotions, mental thoughts, and physical sensations to pass through you, so that you may return to a state of balance over and over again. Only some of the seven billion humans on Earth are actively honoring the choice to create possibilities of a more harmonious reality, because most have sunk into habitual patterns of fear. You, the light movers, are essential in supporting the evolution of all. To do the work you are here to do, you must shake off the malaise of fear. You are here to bring the energy of Home to the planet, and you are here to take the planet Home again. It happens simultaneously.

All of the dis-eases of humanity may be healed by bringing your relationships back into balance, where there is an equal exchange of energy and a flow between give and take. This balanced flow of energy can heal the splits within and between you. Whenever you do *anything*, apply the Golden Rule and think of how what you are doing affects that relationship. The concept of "I am another yourself" (InLak'Ech) applies to *everything*, for everything is energy. Each human must assess how he or she is navigating the energies that are part of the universe by looking at and taking responsibility for your relationship with your own energy. How you work with and utilize energy determines your flow of balance or imbalance within the cosmos.

Humans can no longer continue to believe that you are separate from universal energies that are arriving for your evolution at this time. You are being guided to remember *how* to combine opposites to complement one another to create more harmony. The universal power of unity is stronger than and surpasses your third-dimensional views of varying parts of the whole. If you continue to make choices that keep you in separation, your relationships will reflect the polar opposites of duality. When you feel enough discomfort from the tension of opposites, you will instinctively move to create a change. On Earth, you have the power of *choice* to help you move from separation towards unity.

The experiment of duality is about humans having and correctly using the power of choice. You are granted the right to feel peaceful. All positive things are available to you if you will but *choose* them. Choose to relate only in the state of love.

See others who stand in front of you as part of yourself. You are dis-eased by not loving yourselves and by allowing your expectations and your disappointments to rule your thoughts, rather than choosing thoughts and feelings that resonate with your natural harmonious state of love. Look at your pain and begin to see what causes it. Understand that what you focus on expands; focus on the spirit of InLak'Ech in all your relationships, rather than focusing on the differences that have kept you separate.

You have fables and tales of a Garden of Eden where everything is perfect. We tell you, Dear Ones, that the Garden of Eden is a *state of heart*. You call peace a state of mind, but we call it a state of heart; it is an understanding that everything is as it *should* be, and if there are challenges, then you must simply love them until they pass. Relating to your challenges with feelings of acceptance will allow them to pass more quickly. If you look for the gift in the challenges, then you will see that they are helping you to grow. If you focus on feeling that others are unfair to you or that the universe is unfair to you, you lose the energy of harmony. Because you have forgotten how powerful you are, it is easier for most humans to trust something outside of themselves, hoping that it will fix them, than it is to look inside and trust that *you* have the ability within you to do whatever is required to make necessary changes. Begin to trust in yourselves, and trust that everything is unfolding as it should; this allows you to have a good relationship with the universe.

The opportunity for change is now, for the waves of energy supporting the raising of consciousness are increasing tremendously. Remember that love and light will show you how to move into harmonic resonance in the ways that you relate. Life is a wonderful, harmonic blending of all energies. When you chose to relate through unconditional love with *each* energy that touches you, you free yourself from all the fears that have kept you separate and all the pain and suffering that has been caused through your belief systems. Begin to understand how to love yourselves. See that you and we are one and the same, all connected through divine Source. You are stepping into the Golden Age. It is a process. You have the power of choice to move *with* that process by choosing to relate with the energy of love in every present moment.

We will end this chapter by sharing an experience in relating as described through an enlightened human perspective. Cullen and Pia agreed to meet two friends in the etheric realm. After their experience, Cullen had this to share:

"Immediately as we set the intention to enter into the etheric realm together, my physical eyes began to water, and tears rolled down my cheeks. I felt as though my tears were transporting me into the space of deeper connection. Through my experience of being connected in the etheric, I felt the rolling movements that Laarkmaa describes as the waves of Who We Are. It felt to me like a liquid connection of reaching out and moving towards one another. I now realize what happens when I am tearing with the joy of connection that we can all experience as we move into unity together."

InLak'Ech.

Chapter Seven

THE SEVEN COMPONENTS OF HEALING

"Here on Earth you have seven magical components you may use for healing."

What is Necessary for Healing

We have given you a look at the various aspects of yourselves and how you operate in third-dimensional illusionary reality, and we have told you that to heal the human condition, you must simply remember Who You Are. We will now describe seven components of healing that are necessary to awaken you into a full state of remembrance. Combining your understanding of these seven components with the eight rainbow vibrational essences (discussed in the following chapter) creates a foundation for abundant health.

We will explain each component in detail now.

Energy

We explained to you in the beginning of this book that energy is *everything*, and *everything* is energy. It is as simple as that. Energy is everything that exists. Nothing in physical or etheric form can exist without the presence of energy. You call things into physical manifestation through accessing and shaping the movement of energy. Energy is life; life is energy!

There is nothing else to say about energy that we have not already discussed.

Movement

The secondary component of healing is movement. In order for you to understand how to heal, you must remember that energy always moves. *Life is movement.* You must remember that you are not static, solid beings, but you are energy that continually moves as you respond to, react to, and co-create with other waves of energy. As your energy touches or bumps into another form of energy, you meld and blend with that energy to create a *new* energy. Each of you has been moving around as though you are separate, solid, physical particles. You bump into others that you perceive as also being solidified particles, unaware that you are not solid at all; you are waves of energy. Because you are waves of energy, you are *always* moving, even when you perceive yourselves as being still. As you become more aware and understand yourselves as waves of energy rather than as static energetic particles, you can begin to consciously merge and blend your energies. Remember that each of you is a beautiful, brilliant aspect of your individual self *and* a part of the whole.

Awareness and movement are required to help you continually stay in the present moment. You have become stuck in density through your belief systems, your judgments, and your fears. In order to heal, you must become "unstuck" by simply beginning to see yourselves as constant, flowing energy (movement). *You must be willing to move.* Your mental bodies, your emotional bodies, and your physical bodies are all *moveable.* Stop seeing yourselves as individual particles who hold specific beliefs. Surrender the judgments that create suffering through separation, and be willing to *move* into the flow of possibilities. As you allow yourselves to be more fluid, to move more and more, you will begin to notice that everything else is continually and simultaneously moving. You will become more aware of movement in yourselves and in your environment, and begin to sense the constant movement of life. It can be a little disorienting at first when you become aware of the dynamic and constant nature of movement. As you become less stuck in who you *think* you are, you will remember that movement is also about freedom. You are free to interact with *all* energy in a positive way as you make more and more positive choices in your lives. Exercising choice to always move towards love and light facilitates healing on all levels.

Water

Now that you better understand the role of movement in relationship to energy, you are ready to examine the third component, water. As we have already explained, you yourselves are made primarily of water. As you begin to realize that even your bones are fluid and that every aspect of *you* can move into something *more*, and as you begin to relax your rigid thoughts and beliefs about your perceived reality (including and *especially* your concepts about yourselves), the boundaries that have held you in certain patterns of rigidity begin to dissolve. When you begin to flow with the understanding that everything is *moving energy*, you move more into a true understanding of the possibility of existing in waveform. Observing how water moves gives you a more complete awareness of wave motion and Who You Are as waves of energy.

We have spoken in great depth about water and its magical properties of communication and transportation. As you begin to realize that you are constantly moving energy, you may have physiological sensations of feeling a little "seasick" or dizzy. Once you become accustomed to the feeling of continual movement, you may begin to feel like you are floating through your life, very much here and present in the work you are here to do, but also lighter, without so much influence from the forces of gravity. You will be simultaneously and equally aware of the freedom of wave motion and the effects of gravity in your third-dimensional experience.

Awareness of the rhythm of your physical heartbeat and the flow of your blood, like water, connects you with the flow of universal rhythms. Your etheric form moves in harmony with this universal flow. As you become more aware of your own physical movement, you will better connect with your etheric bodies. (We will say more about this in a moment.) Water is essential as an element of healing in more ways than you can imagine. As you awaken to Who You *truly* Are, you will understand that you can always be forms that flow in waves, fluid and able to move, change, or transcend whatever comes your way.

Light

Light is the fourth component necessary for healing the human condition. You may see light and fire as the same or very similar energies. Light from the universe enters through your solar plexus; when you feel that connection, you experience joy. When you feel disconnected from universal light and from each other, your stomachs hurt, and you cannot feel the state of joy. Is there any doubt why so many of you so often experience stomach distress? You are light beings; you come from love and light, and as beings of light, you are here on a planet of duality to bring that light into the denseness of the third dimension. We call you light movers because of the way you can work with light. Guided by your will, light moves your intentions to your heart centers and then outwards to all other beings in the universe. As light comes to you from the universe and you give your light back to the world, you create a constant flow of energy that moves you towards higher and higher levels of consciousness. Light works in a pattern of swirling energies.

You are also *intended* to use your vision as an aspect of light. You are *intended* to see the light of each other's hearts through what is reflected through your eyes. You are *intended* to reflect light from your hearts through your eyes to connect with others and raise the vibrations between you. However, most of you shield your true sight, looking only with your third-dimensional eyes most of the time, and seeing only what is visible through your filters of experience, thoughts, and beliefs. You have created a veil formed from your thoughts and beliefs that dulls all of your awareness, preventing you from seeing the true reality, which is always in front of you. This veil (which from our perspective is an illusionary filter) changes your perspectives and separates you from universal reality. You see obscurely, as if you are looking through a fog or through thick glasses; such obscured vision causes you to judge what you see. You are not intended to use your vision in this way; it is intended to be used to shine the light that emanates from your hearts through your eyes. You are only able to see the light shining out of one another's eyes when you are connected to Source and can radiate love from your hearts.

We know about your concept of "the magic mirror," which supports a *belief* that you should reflect to others what they need to work on, or what you perceive is out of balance. We find this concept *completely* backwards. You can only find what is out of balance by looking *within* yourselves. It is not your job to reflect your view of what someone else needs to work on as seen through your own limited human filters, beliefs, and perceptions. You must learn to look beyond these filters and to see with the light of love; when you do this, the distortions and the filters of the third-dimensional world are removed, the veil drops, and you are more able to properly use the concept of mirrors, reflecting the light of who a person truly is, for then you are more connected with Who *You* Are. When you look at another, if you shine the light from your heart through your eyes, they can see a better reflection of who they *truly* are through what you reflect. When each person receives a reflection of who they truly are, the brilliance of that light enables them to move beyond their own limited perspectives.

Remember, your vision is not limited to the third dimension only. Please, Dear Ones, remove the veil of separation from your eyes and begin to see the light of Who You Are. You can no longer remain in the current forms you have created, for Earth is ascending, and if you wish to go with Her, you must raise your vibrations beyond the confinements of your third-dimensional vision. Using light to *truly see* is essential to healing the human condition. Remove the barriers of your misperceptions and begin to reflect the light that you are. All aspects of light reflect love—*All.*

Sound

Sound is the fifth component of healing that you must understand. Sound is powerful energy that begins the process of manifesting reality. We spoke earlier about how you "speak each other into being." This is accomplished through sound vibrations. Sound is an important component of healing. How you utilize tones and how you speak words filled with those tones creates the energy that shapes and forms you and everything around you. When you use your will to focus your thoughts and intentions, directing your thoughts through your hearts, you may properly use your heart's wisdom to direct the power of sound to *speak* those thoughts into being. One of your creation myths tells you, "In the beginning was the Word." That concept could be more accurately expressed as, "In the beginning was sound," for it is sound that gives power to the intentions and the thoughts that create the reality you experience. What you manifest in your reality emanates from sound.

Sound is the primary element in causing physical manifestation. We have told you that everything is energy and that energy is continually moving. The energy of everything is constantly moving first into waves of etheric manifestation, and then into waves of the physical, and finally into waves of the two joined together. Sound is the prime mover. Your reality is largely determined by how you transform your thoughts into sound. Resonant energies combine through sound to manifest form. Proper use of sound can help you to create a better world. You are now actually able to hear more universal sounds than you are aware. Learn to become more quiet and still your thoughts to listen to the sounds of the universe. Cosmic sounds, the sounds of the universe, can help you to co-create a multidimensional reality that is fuller, richer, and more harmonious than the third-dimensional reality you currently experience, which has been created through sounds of conflict, fear, judgment, and various other sounds of discord. Even your music (or sounds you *think* are music) contributes to how you manifest your reality.

As the process of ascending into multidimensionality accelerates, you may even begin to *hear* the sounds that propel the movement of manifestation. Begin to focus on sounds that are pleasing, harmonious, and full of love, for these sounds will help you in opening to the true essence of Who You Are as human beings, healing yourselves from the fears and worries that you have carried throughout your lives. You may participate in manifesting a more positive reality here in the third dimension, *if you choose.* In order to enhance the process of healing, it is time to stop the use of disharmonious sounds. It is time to unravel the negative things that you have spoken into being, and to heal how you have harmed yourselves through the negative thoughts that you have *voiced.* Begin to use the power of sound to create a resonance that will allow you to hear higher dimensional vibratory communication. *We* communicate with such higher vibratory sounds, and *we* represent a clear example for you to remember that *you* can, too. In the spirit of InLak'Ech (which means "I am another yourself"), we *are* you; we are the same, and as soon as you begin to remember this, you will also be able to have the joy and the bliss of this experience.

We would like to facilitate your ability to communicate with one another as we do, without the use of technology. It is possible for you to move beyond *all* technology, and learn how to communicate simply, heart to heart. We call the expressing of your energy by speaking your name communicating through heart songs. Your heart song is the signature of your essence; it is a sound that expresses who you are. Our heart song is Laarkmaa (pronounced Laaaaarkmaaaaa). Speak our heart song and let that song penetrate into your own awareness; *feel* the energy of our presence within your being. You may be able to understand how you communicate the essence of Who You Are by simply voicing your name. As you become more adept at reading energy, listening to one another's heart songs will allow you to learn and share a great deal about who each of you is and what you wish to communicate. Your heart songs carry more of your personal energy than other words you speak. Your heart songs and other words and tones send messages of vibratory movement throughout space, without the need for technology. As you continue on your evolutionary path, you can expand your use of sound vibration to carry essential messages. Once you understand that everything is energy, that energy has intelligence and is always moving, and that sound is the prime mover of energy, you need to understand only two more very important components to heal yourselves.

Nature

The sixth component of healing is the understanding of and participation with Nature. In your third-dimensional physical reality, you have almost completely ignored and separated yourselves from Nature. So many people look at artificial representations of Nature through photographs, television screens, or on Internet screen savers where you can see virtual pictures of trees, forests, water, and animals. Rather than simply looking at a "virtual reality," you need to take walks outside, get your feet wet, feel the wind, the sun, and the ground under your feet. You simply cannot receive an energetic exchange from an artificial source; you can only find that *directly* in Nature. It is supremely important that you understand your interaction as part of Earth and part of Nature, for you *are* Nature and Nature *is* you.

You have stepped away from Nature through completely placing all of your energy into technology, because you *believe* that the mental concepts that have developed technology are greater or more important than the truth that lives within Nature. You have given up your natural rhythms that connect to Nature, substituting them with artificial light, too many work hours, and especially, living with too much speed. You have sped up your neurological patterning so much that it is impossible to remain healthy because you are pushing your bodies' neurological systems past their natural, harmonious rhythms. You have caused your bodies and your minds to expend energy in ways that create dis-ease. You are not receiving the natural benefits that Nature provides by looking at artificial images of Nature on your television screens, your computer screens, or even in beautiful photographs. You do not receive the benefits of the restorative and healing elements that you need from a true experience of Nature through these artificial representations, nor do you honor Who You Are as part of Nature.

Examples of separating yourselves from natural rhythms include doing such things as working through the dark rather than sleeping. Working and being active during the night is not harmonious with Earth's natural rhythms (which are *your* natural rhythms, too), and has caused you to become more and more disconnected. Furthermore, to sustain these artificial rhythms, you make choices to ingest artificial stimulants (such as caffeine, sugar, and nicotine, which spike your energy), so that you can continue to function at an artificial pace. Then when your systems become so stressed and tired from this constant, unnatural speed, you ingest substances (such as alcohol or drugs) to artificially relax your systems and slow you down. Keeping yourselves in this pattern of artificial stimulation and relaxation completely destroys your natural rhythms and keeps your bodies and minds in a confused state.

Once you have reached this untenable state through using artificial substances to govern your pace of living, you become more and more dependent upon these substances to maintain the rate of your so-called optimal productivity, and it becomes extremely difficult to reverse these patterns. In the end, you are getting nowhere, because these artificial impingements upon your natural physical states cause you even greater disjointedness, disconnection, discomfort, and dis-ease. When you are out of harmony with Nature, you do not participate with life as intended. In order to heal, you must live within the beneficial and healing rhythms of Nature.

Nature is your primary teacher on Earth. When you step out of balance with Nature, you create a sense of being out of control in your lives. Once this process is started, you continually find it necessary to try to control everything in your environment. You begin to ignore and dismiss your own natural rhythms through living at an artificial pace against your natural flow, until you move further and further towards dis-ease as we have just described. In so doing, you lose contact with the natural self-correcting rhythms that Nature teaches you, and you create conflict in everything. Eliminate this source of conflict, and you will have mastered an essential element in your healing. We are now ready to reveal the final, seventh component necessary for healing the human condition.

Liquid Time

The seventh component consists of correcting your misunderstanding of the illusionary system called "time." Time focuses on past and future, two opposites that separate you from the eternal present. You have allowed your minds to categorize all of your experiences into compartments relating to something other than the present moment. You align all of your experiences, your emotional hopes and fears, and your habitual thinking, with categories that do not exist; there is no *category* that can contain an illusion of past or future, because they don't exist! As you raise your consciousness and increase your awareness, you will begin to perceive that the true flow of the eternal present is liquid.

The illusion of time that you have created will begin to dissolve as you develop a sense of the liquid flowing of energies, rather than static categories of past or future. The past is finished and old, while the future does not exist because it has not yet happened. As you drop away from your beliefs in time, your perceptions of past and future will begin to flow into and out of the present moment until you can no longer distinguish between them. In other words, there will be no barrier between occurrences; they become fluid. Things that you have held in your mind as "past" may present themselves to you in this present moment, and things you have held in your mind as "future" may also appear in the present. Your perception of time will become very liquid for you as the entire structure of time dissolves into the potency of the present. Cullen and Pia have already begun to have such experiences of Liquid Time, and we have asked them to share examples of those experiences here:

Pia: I walked by the living room on the way to the kitchen and noticed Cullen sitting in a chair. He then disintegrated before my eyes and was not there at all.

I immediately called to him and asked if he was in his physical body. Instead of responding from the living room where I had just seen him disintegrate, Cullen answered me from downstairs. He was *not* in the living room *at all* where I had just seen him, although I *knew* that I had seen him there seconds before. The experience of seeing Cullen and talking to him in that chair had actually occurred the day before, and yet fragments of that experience were "showing up" on the next day. There is no way to explain this except to say that time *truly* does not exist.

Cullen: I experienced noises in the house as though someone were walking in a room above me. I called out to Pia to see if she was walking around or making noises above me, and she answered from a *completely* different part of the house. From what I was hearing, I was *sure* that she was directly above me in that instant, as she had been in "real time" the day before. This leads me to the conclusion that time as we know it is no longer accurate or even relevant to our experience.

Viewing your experiences from the perspective of parallel dimensions (which we have previously discussed) is more consistent with universal truth than insisting on seeing life as a linear progression called "time." We call this fluid view of life Liquid Time because the concept of time becomes very fluid when you begin to integrate the possibility of parallel dimensions into your understanding.

If you will remove your misunderstandings about time and the categories of time that keep you living in an illusion, you will begin to see the energetic movement of everything flowing together. Time becomes liquid and you will begin to see a liquid flow of energy, which is life energy, moving in wave form. If you listen deeply to your hearts and the cosmos, you will discover that energy is moving *continually*, and everything happens in the here and now.

We have given you the seven components of healing (listed here) to stretch your remembrance and remove all of the things that keep an illusionary veil of separation between you and the *true* reality.

Seven Components of Healing:

1 ~ Energy (All That Is)

2 ~ Movement (dissolving of structure)

3 ~ Water (fluidity, creativity, communication, transportation)

4 ~ Light (fire, inner light, sun)

5 ~ Sound (vibrational tones, speaking yourselves into being)

6 ~ Nature (everything on Earth, life's rhythm, flow)

7 ~ Liquid Time (parallel dimensions, space)

Each human has the capacity to heal herself at any given moment if she understands and implements all the energetic components of healing. While other humans can offer their support and perspective, actual healing can *only* be accomplished by each individual. Using these components and integrating them at a cellular level will awaken you into deep remembrance so that the human condition can be healed finally, fully, and completely. This is our gift to you who have chosen to be here now to elevate the consciousness of humanity and to support the Earth's ascension. You and only *you* can accomplish this. Each of you will have to make the choice to take your own responsibility to do what you came here to do. If together you make this choice, you will bring the energy of Home into Earth, and you will take planet Earth Home!

Chapter Eight

A RAINBOW
OF HEALING
ESSENCES

*"Achieving a Rainbow body is a
possibility for each of you, when you
continually make conscious choices."*

The Rainbow Body

Healing the human condition and healing the planetary condition require a greater understanding of the energies of light, sound, emotion, thought, and the physical world, and how they interact together. The Rainbow body is created when you learn how to integrate all of these elements and join your light body forms (etheric forms) and physical forms together. Most of you focus primarily on the physical form. In terms of healing, your focus shows up as concerns about symptoms, pains, and the discomfort of dis-ease. You need to be aware that a very real etheric-physical connection exists in order to work with it for your own healing. We have written previously of how the etheric and physical bodies connect. We will summarize this information again here.

The etheric body is the blueprint for your physical form. All physical conditions manifest from that etheric blueprint. How the etheric *shapes* and *forms* your physical body is directed by the energy you project into the etheric field through your thoughts and emotions. If you wish to have healthy, functioning physical bodies, you must have healthy, functioning, positive thoughts, rather than negative, worried, or fearful thoughts. In order to be healthy, your thoughts must be powered by the feeling state of *love* rather than by emotions fueled by fear. When your thoughts become negative because they are paired with emotions (all of which are fear-based), those thoughts travel into the etheric to negatively manifest the physical world. Humanity receives negative or positive vibrations individually and collectively; both the person sending and those receiving the energy of such thoughts and feeling states experience the impact of either negative or positive energy in the etheric body, which then reflects it into the physical body. Both positive thoughts with feelings of love and negative thoughts with emotions are sent as vibrations to the etheric first and reflected back into the physical. The etheric *always* reflects back what it has received.

A person sending out emotions of anger, rage, worry, despair, or fear, damages his or her own etheric form and the etheric forms of others. Those vibrations travel *first* to their own etheric body; they are then projected either onto an intended target, such as another person, or released into space, which affects *every-one*. Such behavior projects negative holes into the etheric aura, imprinting a dark space on your own etheric blueprint, which then radiates back to your physical body in the form of physical imbalances that can manifest as dis-ease. (Whether it manifests as individual dis-ease in others depends upon their personal choice and attitude. Each person must take responsibility for and respond or react to the energy that is presenting itself.)

Imbalance begins when the etheric body is separated from the joy vibration that is your natural state, the one into which you were born. You suffer *so* much illness because you are not aligned with your natural feeling states, which you have forgotten. In your simplistic third-dimensional misperceptions of cause and effect, you have forgotten these broader concepts. Open your hearts to remember how the etheric body and the physical body relate to one another. By doing so, you are opening your awareness and taking responsibility to create a Rainbow body, which is a fully functional blending of your etheric and physical forms. When you vocalize your thoughts, the effect is magnified; when you power words with your feeling states (whether through the negativity of your emotions or the positive feelings of joy, trust, love, and compassion), the effect is amplified *exponentially*. It is important for humanity to understand the dynamic interplay and the vibrant possibilities for co-creating health. By learning to manage the flow of energies between the physical and the etheric, those positive vibrations you send to the etheric will freely flow back into your physical bodies to create better health and to begin to form a Rainbow body. A fully formed Rainbow body is completely healthy!

As an example, when you experience a chronic pattern of worry, you send forth the vibration of worry to your etheric form and into the etheric of the collective. That low vibration is then reflected back to the physical. Normally each part of your physical body communicates with all of the other parts, with trust that each part will perform its job as it should. When you inject worry or fear, you undermine the natural trust that causes everything in your physical to flow in harmony. Once that trust is eroded, the connections begin to break down; in an individual, the organs stop functioning properly and tissues may become dis-eased because communication does not flow in a state of trust and balance as it is designed. The collective receives these lower vibrations as well, eroding the trust that supports unity, causing a collective manifestation of more illusions based on fear and distrust.

Projected grief or anger also enters into the individual and the collective etheric, reflecting to and lowering the physical vibrations of everyone. Worry and frustration do the same thing. If not responsibly used to guide you back into harmony, *all* negative feelings of anger, grief, jealousy, fear, hatred, and other emotions can place a dark spot on the etheric that eats away the etheric field like acid. Then the etheric body reflects back dark spots to your physical forms that cause you to feel torn and imbalanced. This interactive pattern affects the manifestation of everything physical. It reflects as personally dis-eased human states and collective dis-eased human conditions such as war and violence. If you continue the same thought patterns, the spots become larger. The spots on the etheric begin to fade and heal when you choose to positively change those thought patterns, yet it takes *consistency* to make permanent changes. This process does not happen instantly. The etheric naturally will reflect wholeness and health to your physical forms when you consistently feed it positive thoughts and feelings. It is at this point of healing that you may begin to manifest your Rainbow body.

You will not automatically injure your etheric form if you have a negative reaction to circumstances. Instantly correcting your reaction prevents damage. Yet if you *persist* in falling into negative reactive patterns over and over again without correcting them *instantly*, it will take a much greater effort to correct a dis-eased problem. It is important in human healing to understand that you do not have to be *perfect*; you need to learn to be *consistent* in returning to a point of balance. Perfection is *not* part of the third dimension, although we smilingly tell you that you are perfect *when* you consistently take responsibility for changing patterns that do not serve you. Begin to flow towards positive thoughts consistently until they become a regular part of you. When you remember that you can respond at light speed to any emotional nudge to change your thoughts, you can correct the trajectory of negative thoughts instantly. This action will stop the movement towards your etheric *before* the thoughts can cause any damage. Learn to govern your thoughts and pair them with appropriate feeling states. In this way you may manifest greater health and healing in the physical body.

Your goal is to meld and merge your etheric and physical forms together, so that your energy flows back and forth until there is no barrier between them. This free flow of energy then reflects Who You Are as a healthy human, a light mover, and one who is manifesting the possibilities of living in a Rainbow body. You may envision this somewhat like Peter Pan's sewing on his shadow.

Use light and sound to correct negative thoughts and negative emotions. Visualize light as colors or go outside and physically look at Nature's colors. Look at colors in the sky at sunrise and sunset, seeing the colors as radiant light and life. Use sounds. It takes uplifting, higher vibrational sounds, not disruptive, jangling noises, to soothe and elevate the human spirit. The musical forms many of you choose (such as rock, rap, jazz, or country music) disrupt human brain patterns and lower the spirit; those sounds bring the opposite of what you want to feel. Disjointed rhythms disrupt harmonious functioning of the physical form. If you listen to irregular sounds and irregular beats, you will have chaotic thoughts, and your body will not function in harmony with its natural rhythms for optimum health. If you are listening to dissonant noises that disrupt brain function, we suggest you choose instead to listen to sounds that resonate with calm, peace, and joy. Choose more balanced rhythms of musical sounds to connect you to the rhythm of the your own heartbeat and brain waves and enhance your rhythmic resonance with Nature. Your etheric form benefits from listening to sounds that are soothing and calm. Sounds that are in rhythm with your own heartbeat support your physical bodies. Choose musical sounds that positively affect both your physical and your etheric to support the creation of your Rainbow body.

We have noticed that many humans pair consuming alcohol and listening to disruptive music. You often surround yourselves in chaotic environments such as your bars and your clubs, listening to unsettling music. Listening to teen-age music (some of which is extremely chaotic), to rap (which is aggressive and harsh), to country (which carries lower-vibratory emotional tones), or even to jazz that has irregular beats and odd rhythms, causes harm to your physical body both through brain wave dis-function and heart dis-regulation. Many of you blindly reach for alcohol to sooth the disharmony you have created through listening to these dissonant and disruptive sounds. The reason you like certain disruptive patterns of sound is because they are *familiar* to you in the third dimension. However, familiarity is not necessarily a good thing. Until you become more familiar with your natural feeling states of love, trust, and joy, be careful of choosing things just because they *seem* familiar.

Now many of you are struggling with intense emotions; emotions are arising because you need to release old patterns of thought and behavior and replace them with newer, healthier ones. Emotions have a purpose but should not be linked to negative thoughts. You need to understand the simple concept that if you think negative thoughts, those thoughts move like arrows into your etheric forms, ripping them apart. The etheric body then reflects a dis-eased state back to the physical because of the damage the etheric has received from the negative thoughts. We trust that you understand what we are saying because we say it over and over again.

New patterns need to be established that enlarge the connections between your etheric and physical, so that you may begin to function with light flowing back and forth in unity. Because you have not been using your intuition or First Sense regularly, a part of your brains has atrophied. We are referring to the pineal gland that transforms light into a usable form of energy. Without the full use of the pineal gland, your minds and hearts do not function well together. You make choices according to what your mind *thinks* is best from experience and history, rather than allowing your First Sense to guide you in the present moment. Relying on what you know from your experience will no longer work; it will only give you a false sense of comfort of believing that you know what to do next. We implore you to hear us: it is a *false* sense of comfort, for nothing is or will be as it was. There is no constancy in what *was*, for the old is falling away and dying, and the new is being born; it is not yet here. So if you rely on the old, you are clinging to old patterns that will continue to cause you further and further dis-ease and ill health.

Some of you may think that it is much easier to be out of a physical body, but we tell you that is not the truth. The etheric world *does* have fewer restrictions than the restrictions you feel in your physical bodies, but when you are able to properly meld your physical and etheric bodies together, you will exponentially increase your ability to experience joy and pleasure! Challenges are increasing to enhance your understanding of how you may move back and forth between the etheric and the physical *at will* in the form of a Rainbow body, so that you may experience something heretofore only imagined. Having both a healthy human body that allows you specific functionality and a light body that allows you travel without the physical body (if you so choose) will be of great benefit to you. To meld these forms together, you must diligently work at ridding yourself of dis-ease and returning to balance over and over and over again.

You need to begin to act from the intuition provided by your hearts, rather than *thinking* about what you should do next. Your hearts will never lead you astray. Begin to honor and use your First Sense; this will open the portal of your pineal gland to receive more light. Allow the incoming light to guide your way and support your process of change. The more you do this, the greater the connection between your physical and your etheric, and the easier you will flow into your Rainbow body.

Know this: what you project, we *all* feel. This is one reason we wish to help you, because you affect the equilibrium of the entire universe with your thoughts and feelings. We do not complain; that is not our nature. But we want you to know that what you are doing is harming yourselves and others, and we are here to help you change that.

A Rainbow of Energies

Now we will explain to you the rainbow of color essences and how to use them to create your Rainbow body. If you experimented with any of the exercises we provided in Chapter 5, you have already begun to better understand the potency and power for change that is present with the use of the energies of color. To further your exploration of the rainbow of color energies, we will now present you with eight essences of energetic vibratory color to use for your healing, growth, and expansion. We have already given you seven specific components of healing. Together, these eight essences of vibratory color and the seven components of healing combine to create a vibration of six, which represents flow. (7 + 8 = 15; 1 + 5 = 6. This numerical energy is consistent in both your understanding of digital Earth numerology and in Pleiadian, universal mathematical expression.) The energy of six, which represents flow, will help you to create your Rainbow bodies as you remember and flow into Who You Are: divine waves of love and light.

Humans tend to see things linearly, in a progressive order. Because of this, we often present colors to you in various orders for various purposes. Each order has a particular flow that helps you to understand relationships between the color energies. One order is presented in our Heart Meditation (presented in Chapter 5 of this book). We will now give you a similar, yet slightly different, presentation to help you understand how you may use the color essences for healing. Here, we will relate each color to a numerical understanding of energy. Even though we are giving you a linear pathway to follow, please remember that life does *not* move linearly; it *spirals*. Nevertheless, you may follow the sequential order to find your own rhythm of moving within the spiral. Enjoy these energies to assist your growth. As we describe each color's energetic essence, *feel* the energy of that color in your heart and hold it in your mind to take in the fullness of its intended purpose.

Each of the colors we discuss has already been described in *Conversations With Laarkmaa.* We are going to expand your understanding here, as we explore each color more deeply, and explain its mathematical relationship. You carry all of the eight color energies in your Rainbow body, as well as others that you will become more aware of as you develop. You are drawn to one specific energy or another when you focus on various aspects of yourselves, what you remember, and what you choose to share. Learn to see yourselves as energetic jewels radiating out to others through the individual components that make up the whole.

The first color we wish to explore is pink. Pink relates to the energy of love. Mathematically, pink and love relate to the energy of the number one, for one represents the totality of all. When you are focused on unity, one is all there is, and love is all that matters. The energy of love is everything! Even though situations and circumstances may materialize that appear to be the opposite of love, remember that love can unify everything. So pink is an energy that carries the form for oneness and love in the universe. You can, if you choose, relate the color pink to heart energy.

The second color is blue. Blue represents the energy of trust. Blue is the color *we* use to represent ourselves to you, coming to you as blue waves of energy, so that you may feel trust in our presence and in what we share. Mathematically and energetically, the number two relates to the split from unity into duality in the third dimension, where the energy of one splits to become two, often causing humans to move from a unified trust into the challenges and difficulty of separation. From our perspective, the energy of trust is mathematically related to two, because it is with trust that you recognize that *each* separate element in duality *is* a valuable part of the whole. When working with this energy, you can trust that any difficulty presented from the energy of two can be moved back into a unified harmony.

We present the blue energy of trust in the second order to assist you in understanding that everything that *seems* separate is simply an individual *aspect* of the whole. Blue is the color that helps you dissolve your beliefs and trust that there is *more* than what you have believed to be true. The more you trust, the more you begin to be able to see that you are not separate and that everyone and everything is connected. Work with this and allow the blue energy of trust to heal everything you have *perceived* as separate.

The third color we wish to present is green, the color often associated with healing, for green represents growth on your planet. On Earth, your grass, trees, and plants are all comprised of green energy, giving off the green colors that you see. Earth's trees and plants carry abundant green energy to be used for your natural support and healing. *Simply* by being in their presence, honoring their essences, and ingesting their gifts, you absorb their healing energy. Mathematically, the energy of three represents creativity, which is aligned with healing and growth. Use the green energy to heal the imbalances of the current human condition and to create a new and greater reality for yourselves. The proper use of green energy will support your developing your Rainbow bodies.

The fourth color we wish to share is gold, which brings the energies of grace and compassion. We place gold in this position because grace and compassion are the energies that dissolve and correct all karma that you have accumulated in the choices that you have made; grace and compassion can help you to create a better world through creating better choices. Employing this golden energy in and around you supports your capacity to be kinder to yourselves and others, and gives you the ability to forgive yourselves (and others) by providing compassion for all. Being in this state of grace allows you to stop resisting anything that is different. As the energy grows within you, you will have more compassion for others. This *increase* in compassion causes you to decrease your *reactions*, allowing you to flow more into harmony. Many, many years ago, Cullen began to speak a simple truth:

"You cannot be in a state of compassion if you are in a state of reaction. Conversely, you cannot be in a state of reaction if you are in a state of compassion."

As you begin to employ the golden light of grace within and around you, enhancing your natural abilities to be compassionate, you will begin to understand that there *is* nothing to forgive. When you see everything through the eyes of grace, there is never anything to forgive because your compassion and grace help you to understand and accept everything that comes to you. By doing this, you will begin to realize that everything has a purpose as it is. The use of this golden energy does much to eliminate judgment and separation. The Golden Rule ("Do unto others as you would have them do unto you") is a formula for applying grace and compassion in daily life. Considered mathematically, the energy of four represents foundation. Use the golden light of grace to help you build and sustain your new foundation of love, trust, joy, and compassion. Living in a state of grace allows you to see and appreciate everything that is.

The color we have chosen to present as the fifth energy is violet (and its deeper shades of purple). We have chosen to place it here because in mathematical terms, five represents the energy of change, and the violet (or purple) energy conveys transformation or transmutation. Transformation occurs by making changes. Violet energy quite naturally follows golden energy, because when you apply compassion to *everything*, it becomes easier to transform through making changes. All manner of things you are working to change, transform, or transcend can be alchemically altered through the use of violet energy. Use it to transcend challenges or difficult situations. Use the golden and violet energies together and discover how potent they are! Transcending your current belief systems with the support of these energies will help you remember your true state.

We place the energy of white in the sixth place. White carries the energy of truth and universal knowing. The Christ light has been described as an intense white light that opens you to see the truth. The energy of white can feel very strong because it breaks apart your illusions. White is the unity of the all-knowing truth. It presents everything in a unified form that helps you to understand and remember the truth of the greater reality of the universe and the truth of Who You Are. Using and surrounding yourselves with white light helps you to cut through all of the illusions and beliefs that have kept you in a state of separation. We have placed white in the sixth position because from a Pleiadian perspective, the energy of six is mathematically related to flow. Some of you who work with the energy of numbers use six to represent the energy of Home. Our intention in relating white to the number six is to help you flow more into being your true selves and to bring Home to Earth.

We present the energy of yellow, which represents illumination, in the seventh place. The mathematical energy of the number seven is related to magic. We see seven's energy as useful for removing the Veil of Illusion, which will help your becoming illuminated. The mathematical power of seven gives you the ability to drop the illusion that a veil even exists, while the yellow energy of illumination helps you *see* how to do this. Yellow energy quite naturally follows the white energy of truth, for once you understand what is true, you become illuminated. It is also yellow energy that gives you the vibration of joy. Once you are fully in contact with the *truth* of remembering that the universe is filled with *love,* you will feel complete and total *joy* in your hearts. That joy is the manifestation of your illuminated state. Yellow energy will help you to become illumined into the full vibrant awareness of Who You Are as human beings.

The eighth color we present to you is silver, which holds the energy of infinity and connection. Silver sparkles like starlight; silver shines like sparkles of light on water. The energy of eight mathematically depicts a perfect infinity loop, and represents the energy of connection and abundance. Silver is a sparkling essence of brilliant light that shows that everything in the universe is connected. You may utilize silver energy to help you weave threads of connection between everything that exists here on the planet and out into the universe. Silver energy promotes your remembrance that everything is energy and *all* energy is infinitely connected in unity. Silver energy can also help you to dissolve your beliefs about time, so that you can better *know* the abundance that is always yours in each present moment. When you *feel* the truth of how abundantly you are connected to everything you need *right now,* you begin to sparkle yourselves!

These eight energetic essences comprise a rainbow of color and energy that support and nurture your physical, mental, emotional, and etheric bodies as you adapt to the influx of light energies pouring into you from the universe. If you use all of these colors in their myriad combinations, at the very least, you will certainly enhance your lives. More importantly, they can be used to help you join your etheric and your physical together to create your Rainbow bodies.

There are other colors within your energetic spectrum that you may use as well. They are important, but they relate more to your third-dimensional experience than to the multidimensionality of universal energy. Red is the energy of life on Earth. It is the energy of movement in all circumstances on Earth. Think of your blood: it is red, and it continually moves to support your physical existence. We find it amusing that in duality, you have completely misunderstood this energy. In some cultures, you actually utilize the color red for road signs to indicate that movement must stop! Enjoy the red energy as a vibrant part of who you are on Earth.

The color orange is a combination of red (movement) and yellow (illumination). These colors merge together to form the energy of protection, which is needed in the third dimension, as you are evolving past duality and separation. You may utilize orange energy at any time when you feel disharmonious or separating energies around you, but it is best used, like all the colors, to match the circumstances moment by moment.

Other colors exist outside of your energetic spectrum. As you awaken, you will become aware of them. They are multi-dimensional colors of luminescence, iridescence, and sparkle. Some of these colors have a metallic quality that you may not yet be able to fully integrate, but as you develop, you will be able to see and work with them more clearly. As you move more fully into your Rainbow bodies, you will become more aware of these other colors. All twelve strands of your DNA will become activated in conjunction with your working with multidimensional colors. Begin now to fully heal yourselves by playing with the eight energies of rainbow essences that we have described to you, integrating other color energies as they arrive. These eight energies will help you move into your Rainbow bodies. We summarize the rainbow energies here for quick reference:

1 ~ **Pink** (love, totality of All)
2 ~ **Blue** (trust, elimination of beliefs, healing the splits of duality)
3 ~ **Green** (healing, growth, creativity, expansion)
4 ~ **Gold** (grace, compassion, new foundation)

5 ~ **Violet-purple** (change, transformation, transmutation)

6 ~ **White** (truth, flow, universal knowing)

7 ~ **Yellow** (illumination, joy, elimination of the Veil of Illusion)

8 ~ **Silver** (infinity, connection, abundance)

Light and color are the same, so when you play with colors, you are moving light. Color energies are attached to every thought you think and travel into the words you speak. When you speak, you bring together light and sound for manifestation. Ask yourselves what energies you place into your thoughts and words, remembering that color is the energy of light and your voice is the energy of sound. Use this guide to enhance your communication. Trust carries the vibration of blue, and love carries the vibration of pink. Giving comes from love, so the quality of giving has pink around it. What vibrations are you placing into your environment? Explore what the energy feels like when you are speaking from your heart or giving a gift or service. What do you experience in a peaceful, meditative state? In meditation, you experience love and truth, transcending all judgment or thought, with no attachment to anything, and so you may become aware of the energies of pink, white, and violet. Golden energy may appear as you feel compassion and grace. You may also become aware of yellow energy, as you experience the joy of illumination in moving beyond the confinement of third-dimensional beliefs and concepts. Within the presence of these energies, you will feel peace, letting you know that everyone is equal, and there is *never* a need for competition. Use the colors of your meditative experience to become familiar with the presence of the energies of pink, white, violet, gold, and yellow. Use violet energy to transcend old beliefs. Open your hearts to trust by combining pink and blue energies, and begin to heal the human condition in the presence of green energy.

Conscious awareness of these energies will guide you as you begin to change your world. Begin to consider the way that you use sound and the light of color to communicate; you can re-write your *entire* language in this way, eliminating all energies of judgment, blame, and separation. Sending love and light is a *very* potent action. Learn to combine the energies of love and light with the energies of sound, and use your divine power to co-create a more harmonious reality. Band together to make a difference. Find a parallel way to live in unity. Find a path that is paved with peace. Remember that love is the most powerful force in the universe; you must simply learn how to be love.

Chapter Nine

ACHIEVING HARMONY

*"When you move beyond the
Veil of Illusion, you will begin
to live in harmony."*

The Three Necessary Elements of Harmony

You have reached a place on your journey where it is important to understand that unity must incorporate all aspects of what exists in the third dimension *and* other dimensions, multidimensionally. Unity requires an appreciation of each aspect as a part of the harmonic whole. Everything that you have read and felt in your hearts so far has been leading you to integrate more and more harmony into the energy of Who You Are. This ninth chapter is about harmony. There are three aspects of harmony, and we wish to focus on each of them. We are presenting this information in the ninth chapter to utilize the energy of nine. From the Pleiadian mathematical perspective, the energy of nine represents the creative energy of three expressed three times to create harmony. That means that the energy of nine offers you all aspects of creativity coming together to coalesce into one unified whole. The three aspects that we will address in this chapter are transparency, androgyny, and community, for without a deep understanding of these three concepts, you will not be able to fully and completely enter into total harmony.

Transparency

Transparency is the act of simply being Who You Are and accepting others as they are. Transparency means that you move beyond the Veil of Illusion, stepping forth without fear of judgment or fear of blame, and without any kind of hidden agenda about what you want or desire. Instead of hiding behind a separating veil, you become willing to be fully present as Who

You Are, joining your energies to others in a borderless realm, for the highest good of all, without attempting to change one another in any way. Living in transparency means understanding that you do not need to change yourselves to please others, nor do you need to change others, for each of you is perfect when you take responsibility for simply being your true selves, loving yourselves as you are now, yet honoring the power to make positive choices for growth in each new moment. The essence of that understanding allows you to feel safe. Humans cannot be fully transparent until you trust and accept the idea that you *are safe* and that everything that happens to you is happening on purpose; you must remember that you are fifty percent responsible for what occurs, for you always have the *magnificent* power of choice. You no longer have to hide behind the illusions of your protective outer personalities, attempting to make people think that you are something other than Who You truly Are.

The outer personality is only one aspect of you. It exists to exhibit your individual gifts and talents. Through bad training, you have learned to use your outer personality as a mechanism to protect yourselves, but that is actually only an artificial way of attempting to insulate you from your fears of being judged or not being loveable. You express your individuality through your outer personalities, but you also hide behind your differences, rather than seeing how you are connected. You use your individuality as a barrier to protect yourselves, but that only separates you from remembering that you are all the same. In stepping away from these illusions about yourselves, you will more easily move towards true transparency. There is no safety in hiding.

As you begin to understand these concepts more deeply, you will begin to realize that there is nothing to fear or hide about yourselves, and that the *only* way to live is to live openly through love. You will begin to feel safe because there *is* nothing to fear;

you will begin to feel safe because you *trust* that everything is proceeding exactly as intended by the love in the universe as the wisdom of your own hearts guides you. That way of living gives you such a basis for trust and safety that there is no need to do anything other than *be* transparent. Transparency means also that you are no longer afraid that you are not loveable, for you begin to see and accept *yourselves* as you truly are. There is no longer a need to convince others that you are loveable, for in transparency, each of you will see the other *exactly* as you are, through vision that is connected to your hearts, seeing the energy that is standing right in front of you, experiencing it, and knowing it through clear and direct sight. You simply *are.*

The vibrations of your essence are transparent, and there is no need to cover or hide them behind illusions of fear. You must be willing to share with one another everything that you have and everything that you are, and you must be willing to receive the gifts of others without judgment, blame, or any ideas of hierarchical superiority. Each of you has brilliant benefits to contribute to the whole, and in understanding and accepting the radiance each of you carries, you create a more harmonious existence. When all barriers of separation and opposition are dissolved, you can achieve the harmony you seek.

Living in transparency also means that you have no real need for communication with words, for when you are being completely transparent, your energy simply speaks through the presence you carry. You have experienced glimpses of transparency in the third dimension. When two humans "fall in love," you drop the illusion of the veil long enough for you to see Who You truly Are. As you recognize and appreciate the truth of Who You Are, you experience joy through closeness and connection. We have referred to "falling in love" earlier in this book, explaining to you how you see the essence of who one another is without any "filterization" of what you wish the other to be, or how you wish the other to perceive you. This is a glimpse of transparency. In order to move into complete harmony, you must begin to live your lives transparently in *every* situation. That means that you must accept the gifts of every person and circumstance as they are presented to you as part of the whole, rather than seeing it as a conflict or challenge.

Transparency means being willing to open your hearts, open your eyes, open your ears, open your feeling states, and open the essence of Who You Are to align with the divine love and light in all others. We repeat this because it is important to remember that you are all connected, and you must begin to accept how each of you contributes equally to the whole. When each of you reaches the level of transparency we are describing, there will be no need for any type of competition or conflict. In fact, you absolutely must eliminate all competition and all conflict in order to reach this level of transparency. When you live in transparency, you will also eliminate all need to control others. The safety of transparency immediately eliminates any possibility of assuming that you can or need to assert your power over another. Instead you gain an appreciation of one other through simply seeing clearly the energy that each of you is.

As you begin to use the concept of transparency, it will enable you to see the rainbow colors of each of you. For example, you may see the color pink, which corresponds with the energy of love, or the color blue, which corresponds to the energy of trust. You may see the color yellow, corresponding to joy, or the energy of green, corresponding to creativity and healing. Using transparency in this manner will allow you to view one another as the Rainbow beings that you are becoming. Of course, as we have explained, it is your choice whether you attain a Rainbow body or not. You have the opportunity to move into Rainbow form through the choices you make, or to prevent your movement into Rainbow form through the choices you *refuse* to make.

You have the choice. But if you choose to moveinto Rainbow form by living in transparency, you will find yourself existing in waveform at a higher vibrational level than you have ever before experienced, because time and the Veil of Illusion will disappear. You will flow towards one another as we do, seeing yourselves in the transparency of moving energy that is present-ing *right now*. You will begin to vibrationally exhibit different colors as you communicate with one another. For example, as you approach another, you may enhance your presentation of blue energy to indicate and encourage an opening of trust between you. Or you may greet each other by showing pink energy, communicating love to one another. You may then vibrationally exhibit the color yellow, representing the joy of connecting through your hearts. And so it goes.

In transparency, you can radiate color energy to one another to enhance clear communication. For example, when you approach another while experiencing a challenging situation in your life, if you are both being transparent, the one you approach will be able to see and feel what *you* are experiencing and will automati-cally know to surround and envelop you in the violet light of transformation and transmutation to support you with your challenge. Likewise, when you approach another transparently and you wish to expand your understanding of something, the one you approach will automatically surround and fill you with the energy of white to enhance your understanding of truth. Can you imagine how this will improve your communication and your abilities to help one another? You will be stepping away from the complications of speech with the ability to communi-cate more directly, as we do. Transparency also eliminates *all* need to filter or censor the truth of Who You Are. You will no longer need to filter what you hear or what you say when you communicate in this way. When you use the vibrations of light and color to communicate in transparency, your communication more easily moves through the water of your physical forms. By accomplishing this, you will have a much greater ability to share your energies more thoroughly, which will bring you closer to unity.

We trust that you understand that it is completely impossible to do any of this until you surrender to trust and accept that you can be safe. Become willing to see all others equally. Be willing to stand naked in the truth of Who You Are in full transparency. When there is equality within love, there is no reason for fear or distrust. Transparency is absolutely necessary to live in unity, and it is the only way that you will ever achieve harmony. If you wish to heal yourselves and heal the human condition, then you must become transparent. Explore the energy of transparency as you rid yourselves of the Veil of Illusion, your systems of belief, your patterns of behavior that have kept you stuck, and all fears that have kept you feeling separated from love and from one another. Explore the energy of transparency moment by moment, becoming more and more transparent as you become more aware of Who You truly Are.

Androgyny

The second aspect of harmony that you must understand is androgyny. The definition of androgyny is the blending of male and female characteristics so that both male and female exist as one. Your current experience in the third-dimensional physical world exists through all of the dualistic splits that we have previously described in this book. One of those dualistic splits is the division of an androgynous whole through the expression of gender. You have experienced conflict, as well as cooperation and unity, through your expression of gender. We have discussed with you how your experience of gender is intended to bring harmony in the presence of love, through merging the different aspects of who you are as male and female. What we wish to discuss now is that *each* of you has an aspect of male energy, the divine masculine, *and* an aspect female energy, the divine feminine, within you in your unified self. The gender you express in each given life predominates your perspective. You are very attached in the third dimension to who you believe yourself to be as a woman or as a man because you see that as your primary identity. You gravitate towards a specific expression of gender according to the physical characteristics you express and your proclivities for that specific gender. Simultaneously, you ignore the influence of the portion of the other less dominant gender that contributes to your total makeup. What we are asking you to do, if you choose, is to accept and understand that each of you is an androgynous being.

We do not mean to alarm any of you or make you feel that you must give up aspects of how you exchange with one another through sexual expression of gender or even how you perceive yourselves as "a man" or "a woman" in the third dimension. These new ideas could become messy in your thinking, so we need to assure you that in accepting your androgynous state, men's penises will not fall off, nor will women's breasts disappear! Rather we wish to expand your joy by helping you understand the truth of Who You Are as androgynous beings. All of these concepts about androgyny are offered to enlarge upon and expand your joyful expression of physical and spiritual love. Sexual expression is only *one* aspect of the beauty of androgyny, yet it is an area that is important to you. We will speak more about the complete understanding of androgyny in a few moments. For now, we will address the sexual aspects in which you are so interested.

As you begin to open your hearts to transparency and are willing to be *fully* seen by one another, your physical expression of sexuality in the third dimension will blossom. We remind you that the expression of sexuality is *intended* to be an offering where you share yourselves completely by joining your physical bodies together though your hearts *first,* allowing waves of physical joy and merging that take you out of separation and into unity. You call this merging "connection" or "orgasm." Through assimilating these ideas, you will begin to experience the expression of love beyond concepts of the mere joining of penis and vagina. Opening to one another in full transparency as androgynous beings will expand the completeness of your "coupling" experiences. Androgyny can be a gateway to move you beyond the limit of your third-dimensional physical sexual experiences. What we are telling you now about stepping into androgyny is a gift, an opportunity to take your third-dimensional expression of sexuality and expand it into multidimensional bliss beyond your current experience or understanding. But it is also meant to help you expand your concepts of Who You Are outside of sexual experience.

Androgyny is about being whole within yourself. While we know that what we say is being integrated through your minds as you read, you will not understand, even though we are giving you energetic stardust to help you assimilate the truth, until you are willing to surrender your own belief systems about who you *think* you are, and are willing to step into the wholeness of Who You *truly* Are. As you begin to accept the totality of Who You Are as an androgynous being, you will have so much more to offer the one with whom you share your heart and physical form here in the third dimension, and all others. With your chosen partner, you will invite a new form of connection and an opportunity for growth, as the two of you expand together in a burst of wave motion, ecstatic fire, and a union of bliss and love that takes you into moments of being beyond the physical experience of orgasm into the multidimensional reality of sharing unconditional love. This joining allows true alchemical, rather than just physical, merging. In relating to all others, you will simply radiate complete, unconditional acceptance.

To heal the human condition, you must move beyond your beliefs about sexual sharing, which so often are ruled more by fear than by love. *Both* men and women are ultimately afraid that if they do not perform through expected sexual roles, *they will not be loved.* That is a basic human fear: the fear that you will not be loved. In fact, the ultimate fear that controls *all* humans is the fear that you will not be loved. To move beyond this fear, you must understand that you are not *losing* something by stepping into androgyny, you are *gaining* something, *and you have choice* in how you do this. You have choice in any given moment of how you wish to share love. *That* is what you are being offered in androgyny: a bliss that is even greater than sexual union, but you do not need to use *only* what we are describing; you may still enjoy the bliss of physical, third-dimensional sexual union, too. You *are* still in the third dimension, and you are intended to continue exploring and understanding the third-dimension. Yet as you develop a multidimensional perspective, you bring the multidimensional experience into your third-dimensional lives, so that you can expand and enhance your experiences, as you encompass greater joy, greater bliss, and greater spiritual and physical connections.

We know that you have concepts of what it means to share love gender to gender, or even within the same gender. We are asking you to stretch those concepts and drop the belief that you are *one* particular gender; you are only the expression of one particular gender in *this* particular third-dimensional experience of *this* moment of *this* parallel life. You are *simultaneously* the expression of other genders in other parallel lives. As you integrate all of your parallel lives together, you move into a greater flow of Who You Are as androgynous whole beings. This now relates to our previous section on transparency.

If you are presenting as an androgynous whole being in transparency, you may then choose how you wish to exchange your energy. You still retain the power of choice. You still retain the power to choose how you want to share love, although once you reach this stage of harmony and understanding, your choice will *always* be to share the totality of Who You Are as a complete Rainbow being. We are not asking you to give up the full expression of your third-dimensional exchanges of heart energy and love. We are simply asking you to consider the possibility, and make the choice to *expand* how you give and receive as you share yourselves with one another. We are describing a form of sharing that has no particular linear direction, but rather shares a moving spiral of life energy.

Androgyny does not refer *only* to human sexuality. A deeper explanation of how androgyny encompasses *all* of the aspects of being female and male will help you to realize how your complete makeup is enhanced through the incorporation of both feminine and masculine qualities. These qualities naturally exist within each of you to bring strength to *both* genders, as both female and male traits are always combined in each of your makeups. Fortunately, while each gender carries specific proclivities that are unique to that gender, it *also* possesses attributes from the opposite gender. This melding of attributes of both genders forms a balance within each of you that creates a fuller and more well-rounded person. Currently, men and women look to one another to find what you *think* is missing within your own gender. In androgyny, you simply must recognize that you carry both male and female gifts within the same personality, which makes you whole and balanced. This is part of what we have been explaining to you about appreciating and honoring the opposites in everything in order to achieve wholeness. Both the feminine and masculine qualities are needed to create a whole and complete human being. What we are explaining here about wholeness with yourselves is *far* more important than what we have explained about sexuality.

Once you begin to accept all aspects of Who You Are, your sense of androgyny will become more and more apparent. You will simply find yourselves always sharing through the energy of love, and you will approach unity with much more joy and completion. Your bliss and your ecstasy will be beyond anything you have experienced, because your experience in the third-dimension is capped, limited by your belief systems, your thoughts, your unresolved emotions, and your attachments to ideas about who you *think* you are. While we are speaking of how to free yourselves into greater inclusiveness of all that you *truly* are (and therefore freeing yourselves from third-dimensional limitations into expanded joy and bliss shared with your chosen partner), we do not advocate returning to the 1960's "hippy" era ideas about "free love." Androgyny does not mean the free expression of sexual love in the third dimension. The third dimension is not conducive to sharing sexual love outside of committed relationships because of existing fears, judgments, competition, and issues of control. Love is, of course, free for all, but sexual sharing is a special exchange of energy reserved for your committed partner.

When you understand yourselves as androgynous beings, you begin to realize that everything you need is within you. An androgynous being is fully aware that you incorporate all aspects of unity within yourself. That realization frees you to fully share yourselves with one another. That means that when you meet another, you will not be looking for something *from* the other. You come together in completion, not from a standpoint of need. Each person who has fully accepted their androgynous wholeness will come to meet you and you will come to meet them through the energy of unity, and it will change *completely* how you share yourselves in love and in all aspects of your lives.

This is androgynous love, and it only becomes available to you when you have done the work to eliminate the illusions that separate you, and most importantly, when you drop away the cycles and patterns of neediness. Androgynous love becomes available when you have stepped outside of the illusion of time, dropping all beliefs about who you *think* you are and eliminating dysfunctional behaviors. You must discard all belief systems that keep you separate, drop all of your fears, and agree to live in the new foundation of love, trust, joy, and compassion. When you build your lives from this foundation and integrate all aspects of Who You Are through transparency and the wholeness of androgyny, you will be able to heal the human condition and step into one harmonic whole, thus creating the possibility for *true* community. We will speak to you about community now.

Community

The third element necessary for understanding harmony is community. Although transparency and androgyny are somewhat new concepts to many, everyone is familiar with the idea of community at some level. The true spirit of community, however, has never been satisfactorily achieved on Earth. You have longed for and tried to attain harmonious communities without great success. Your minds and egos have prevented you from being able to completely create a true sense of community here in the third dimension. Your communities have represented idealized mental concepts that are not lived through the heart, often causing more separation rather than unity. We are going to help you with our perspective to achieve the communities your hearts' desire.

We have watched early humans banding together to work in unity for an entire group. However, we see that because of outside intervention and the injection of fear, you began to group and separate yourselves into individual and opposing tribes and societies that compete with one another, thus creating the dualistic split you currently experience living in the third dimension. Your bad training has taught you that you need to compete in order to survive. Therefore, your ideas about community have moved more and more towards separation rather than unity. These beliefs have become deeply ingrained within your human psyche, erasing anything you might remember about *true* community that once existed in cooperation without cultural identification, borders, religion, or philosophy. You now define community as a gathering together of *only* those who are like-hearted and like-minded into one group that includes those who are *like* you and excludes those who are *not*. Look around you. Evidence is clearly and abundantly visible in communities that are based on religion, race, economic strata, educational attainment, and so many other artificial subdivisions. Even though your hearts remember that the essence of community is based on oneness and unity, community for you has become a concept that *furthers* separation, as you band together those who are *like* you in order to compete with those you perceive as being different. You often seem to perceive the aspect of *difference* as threatening or dangerous, when it is *difference* that helps you to understand and appreciate all aspects of the whole.

One of the largest examples that we can offer to show you how communities have been built upon separation rather than upon unity is to look at your organized religions. Each religion has a separate set of unchangeable belief systems that are exclusive to that religion. You must adhere to these beliefs in order to join that particular community. Each religion also practices hierarchical separation by naming a leader who is supposed to have *special* understanding of the rules or *special* access to God. There is no one religious leader who has direct access to God or Source any more than *each* of you do in your own human hearts.

In fact, if you are relying on others to tell you what divine truth is whispering in your own hearts, you have become too lazy to support your own evolution. Those who do not contribute to their own growth by listening to the wisdom in their own hearts, those who listen *only* to what others say or rely *only* upon words written by someone else, are missing the point.

Divine truth is written within each of you. If you are only reading something someone else has interpreted or written, you are cutting yourself off from your own direct connection with Source. Even if you do not currently *feel* a direct personal connection, the access is always there through your hearts, ready to be re-activated by your intention and your choices. If you cut your connection by always listening to others' guidance, you lose your ability to *know* truth as it resonates within your own hearts. You trade the power of your own direct connection to Source for someone else's leadership or guidance, which can *never* be as strong, true, or direct. The formation of religious communities based on separation can only come from fear and judgment, not love. These communities often judge and condemn others, further separating yourselves, as you struggle under the weight of false belief systems that claim that your community offers the best or *only* acceptable way to live. True community must be open to accepting all aspects of how each of you views the truth. The only guidelines that need to be in place are the ones that we have already suggested throughout this book, and the ones that will be addressed in the tenth chapter. These are the elements of choice. As you suspend judgments and eliminate beliefs, you can create true communities based on love, light, and unity.

We are asking you to awaken as you begin to form communities. You are capable of remembering what it feels like to know that you are safe without having to surround yourselves with only those who appear to be like you. True community cannot exist without all the elements we have so repeatedly explained to you. The way to reach true community can only be found when you are willing to step fully into transparency. You need to build communities that do not have boundaries of family, village, province, state, country, world or any other barriers that you can imagine. Community cannot be achieved when individual egos cling to the ideas of leadership or to the belief that things must be done in prescribed ways. It cannot be achieved by following a guru. You can only achieve true or lasting community by following your own hearts, living transparently, and choosing actions for the highest good of all.

There are groups existing today on your planet that are striving to reach the true sense of community, yet they are unable to achieve it because they still cling to old paradigms that follow rigid sets of rules, regulations, leaders, teachers, and gurus. We tell you, do not even follow *us*. We are not gurus. We simply offer a larger perspective from beyond human awareness, telling you that the only way to achieve unity is through *listening* to your own hearts. Oneness cannot be achieved and community cannot be developed until human hearts awaken to remember that each of you is guided by the same source of love, and that no one person can lead or direct another.

Interactions through competition and conflict between leaders and followers rather than interacting through cooperation will always lead to failure within any community. Communities cannot contain ideas of separation and competition, or hierarchical ideas that one person can lead or control others. A true sense of community requires you to be transparent with one another and share the androgynous whole of yourselves, understanding that you offer and accept everything for the highest good of all. Harmony can only come when you can do this. Peace can only come when you can do this. So you must eliminate all judgment and surrender your belief systems, stop your patterns of dysfunctional behavior that cause you to compete with one another, and begin to step into a true manifestation of cooperation. Not until you simply honor Who You Are and who everyone else is through the spirit of InLak'Ech can this occur. Only leaderless communities can work to achieve this goal.

We suggest that you continue your best attempts to form community, but every time you meet conflict, recognize that the conflict is there in order for you to heal the split of duality as you continue to evolve. Every conflict that comes to you within community is there to show you how to heal it; communities exist to show you how to stop your judgments, how to examine your beliefs, and how to listen to and accept what all others have to offer, while sharing your own thoughts without agenda.

Everything we have addressed about true community will help you in entering into the harmonic whole of unity so that you may experience peace. You are at the gateway of the Golden Age, and the energy of the Golden Age invites the spirit of community for all. By stepping into androgyny and transparency and eliminating all those aspects we have spoken about so often in this book, you will be able to create what your hearts desire and live what you remember about being Who You truly Are. We invite you to do this now, and we suggest to you to remember that you have choice in every present moment. Build your communities from love, by expanding into fully being Who You Are. Remember the Golden Rule to treat others as you wish to be treated. When you base every choice on what is best for everyone, there can be no separation and no hierarchical division. The only thing you need in building community is to understand how to make choices for the highest good for all.

We, Laarkmaa, wish to establish a community here on Earth built upon these principles. We see it as a Center of Love and Light that will be an example where all humans may come to experience harmony in the combined energies of Nature and healthy human interactions in a *real* third-dimensional community that expands to include everything and everyone in love.

Chapter 9 is the last chapter that we will write in this book, although our energy will continue to be present as you read. We have asked Cullen and Pia to write Chapter 10, using the truth that they have remembered from their own hearts about what we have shared.

Chapter Ten

THE TEN CHOICES

*"Now that you know, will you
make the right choice?"*

Guidelines for Living

Laarkmaa has asked us (Pia and Cullen) to write this chapter, and we are pleased to share our viewpoint here. Throughout this book, we have been reminded that because we are human, we *always* have a choice in everything we think, say, or do. We may not *feel* like we have a choice when we are caught up in the dramas of everyday living, but Laarkmaa says choices are always available. We choose our attitudes and our thoughts; we choose to take or not to take responsibility for how we live our lives; we choose which laws to follow (man-made laws or universal laws); we choose our loyalties (loyalty to others or loyalty to our own hearts and the truth); we even choose the manner in which we will ascend, through the traditional process of death by leaving the physical body, as most choose to do, or through moving towards forming a Rainbow body to ascend with the planet. *We have a choice.*

We can choose to cling to our third-dimensional viewpoint of reality, or we can expand our viewpoints to recognize that we are citizens of the universe. We can open our hearts to realize that our true family consists of those with whom we share similar vibrations. We can honor the principle that true loyalty is only respected when we listen to our hearts and follow universal truth as it expresses through our own guidance. Proceeding through daily life believing that we do not make a difference or that things will never change is a choice. We are *not* victims. We choose our reality through every decision we make, and through those that we refuse to make, which is often the largest contribution to reality for most humans. Through fear, we are often frozen and unable to make a correct decision in the present moment.

Laarkmaa suggests that we will make better choices when we abandon our human, mentally-based, logical, decision-making processes and begin to make our choices from our hearts. Laarkmaa repeatedly tells us to listen deeply to what we know in our hearts, for true guidance can only come through when we surrender our fears and *really* trust what is there for us to hear. If we are attached to what we believe, if we place our loyalty towards others before we are loyal to the truth in our own hearts, or if we feel we cannot leave specific places or people that we define as "home or family" through misplaced loyalty, we may miss important signals that guide us to be some "where" else, or more importantly, some "how" else. Our real family consists of other light movers and the beings of light who love and support us, not those to whom we are linked by blood or by law. True connection is made from vibrations of unconditional love. Likewise, Home is not a specific place on the planet; it exists within our hearts, and Laarkmaa has reminded us that our job is to bring Home here to Earth.

Because we have so many questions about parallel lives, healing, ascension, and choice, Laarkmaa has patiently given us a detailed outline of what is required to heal and to ascend with our bodies, telling us that the decision to ascend *with* the body is a commitment to service, and reminding us that only those of us who are dedicated to the *single* intention of releasing all fear, who have the courage to surrender all belief systems, and who are willing to change *everything* in order to be of service to the new earth, will achieve ascension with a full Rainbow body. It is our choice, but we must have a single, fearless and devoted intent in order for that choice to manifest.

The essence of truth in Laarkmaa's messages is that we are safe, and we can trust in the loving flow of the universe. We need only to trust that everything *is* all right. *We* are energy, and waves of universal energy are coming to Earth to meet and support us as we transform. We must simply detach ourselves from any belief systems that involve fear, including our deeply ingrained fear of death. We cannot ascend with our bodies if our sole reason for wanting to do so is that we are *afraid* of and wish to escape death. Likewise, we must choose to support the body if we wish to ascend with it. We cannot live through separate intentions, wanting to ascend with the body, yet also choosing to consume foods or thoughts that harm us and others. Choosing to participate in judgmental thoughts and belief systems, and ingesting harmful food or drinks, contradicts the choice to ascend with the body. Once we know, *we can't un-know* what is the higher choice.

There is no judgment from the universe in a choice to ascend through death rather than to ascend with the body, but, as Laarkmaa has shared with us, choosing to ascend with the body is an act of service and requires the single-hearted intention of trust and acceptance that everything is perfect. With the body, we are able to accomplish more than if we are only existing in etheric form. As Laarkmaa explains, the body is the workplace where we can transmute energy to accomplish more here on Earth. We must recognize that everything is unfolding exactly as it is intended with our participation through the choices we make as co-creators. It is our *job* to step away from all fear and to make conscious choices in every moment. The choice to ascend with Earth is a choice for service, and those who ascend with Earth will do so because they have done the work that is required. Those who choose otherwise, through their ignorance or through disregarding what they know, will have a *different* experience—not bad, negative, or less than, just different. Laarkmaa tells us that they love us, and with that love, they remind us over and over again that we *always* have a choice. Let us join together to choose love and light.

We have noticed that a great deal of what Laarkmaa shares matches spiritual tenets from many different religions. We have selected two of the most common sets of religious guidelines to illustrate similarities with Laarkmaa's teachings. The Christian religion calls their guidelines for living the "Ten Commandments." The Buddhist tradition calls their guidelines the "Noble Eightfold Path of Wisdom." We will briefly look at each of these of guidelines from the vantage point of what Laarkmaa has shared with us. Please notice for yourselves the similarities in these traditional rules for living and the suggestions Laarkmaa has made to help guide us. We will begin with the Ten Commandments.

The "Ten Commandments"

1 ~ Thou shalt have no other gods before me.

In order to step into Who We Are, we must do away with hierarchical beliefs about being connected to God (Love, or Source). God, the one true universal divine energy, is available to *each* of us, and we do not need to place any one person in the position of being *more* divine or *more* knowledgeable about divine truth than any other person. Each individual is part of God (Source); we do not need any other human to intercede for us in our divine connection to God, for each of us is *completely* divine and has direct access to the wisdom of Source without the direction or assistance of a priest, rabbi, or minister. Most, if not all, religions proclaim that there must be a spokesperson or a guru (who is more educated, enlightened, or responsible for interpreting the truth), who is placed at the top of their religious hierarchy to interpret divine wisdom or to control the form of communication between each person and God. This belief system ignores the truth that each of us is able to connect to Source directly. The commandment to "have no other gods before me" becomes cloudy or confused when we choose to follow another's guidance and give up our own power to connect directly with Source. We never need to place another ahead of our own divine connection to Love, Source, God.

Laarkmaa would say: *Choose* **love and your own direct connection to Source.**

2 ~ Thou shalt not make graven images (idols).

Modern technology has taken us to a place where we have created symbols, icons, and many artificial representations or images of life. Through our unquestioning appetite for technology, we have created an idolatrous, artificial lifestyle that we honor as the most important way to learn and communicate. We have stepped away from direct interaction with Nature, confining ourselves to indoor lives that further separate us from the real and natural world. We have stepped away from personal communication, choosing to dash off a few quick words in an email or to communicate through the false idols of Facebook and Twitter, rather than joining another person face to face. We choose a pretty image on our screensavers rather than taking a walk outside. We have even lost, to some degree, our Nature-based language, choosing a language based on technical terms instead (such as speaking about "receiving a *download*," rather than saying that we received spiritual information). Too many of us spend time looking at and "worshiping" artificial images of Nature, rather than spending time outdoors in Nature, communicating face to face with people, and actively participating with life. We need to change our mistaken view of seeing the world through an artificial lens as a virtual reality, and begin to participate with people in a *real* way and with the *real* and natural world.

Modern cultures have also made an idol out of money. We worship money for its own sake, and we have created images that represent money's artificial value. Americans even choose to place the words *"In God we trust"* on the images, or idols, of the highly worshiped dollar. Money has become the most important object of value in our current cultures. We need to step away from that false idolatry of making money the god of success and placing artificial values on it. Our shared gifts and talents need to replace money as the means of exchanging energy together. We must begin to trust that the universe can abundantly provide for us if we only choose to honor and participate responsibly with life.

Laarkmaa would say: *Choose* to trust in what is real and step away from artificially created images of reality.

3 ~ Thou shalt not take the name of the Lord in vain.

Beginning with the premise that each of us *is* God (an individual divine aspect of Source), we cannot treat each other in vain, or in our words, with disdain and disrespect. Thoughts, words, and the tones we use to speak need to be kind and respectful of one another. In each communication, we need to speak as though we can truly see the divinity in each other. We need to move away from thoughts, words, and tones that deliver a message of judgment, blame, or criticism, and choose instead to "speak ourselves into being" by using words and tones that express love and unity.

Laarkmaa would say: *Choose* words, tones, and thoughts that are positive, kind, and respectful.

4 ~ Remember the Sabbath day, to keep it holy.

While each religion guides its followers to set aside one day to honor and remember holy ideas and principles, we feel that in choosing only *one* day as holy, we are missing the truth of how special life is *every* day. Each day should be seen as holy, for each day provides the gift of being here on Earth and offers us opportunities to evolve through the challenges that greet us, and also through the positive things that come our way. We need to honor the truth that not only each day, but each moment can be lived, as a *holy moment,* with gratitude for all that we are given and in appreciation of life. We need to focus on the holiness of each day, rather than saving our reverence for one of seven days that exists in the future, a day that we have meagerly set aside to be grateful or to be "good." We need to remember that we, and all others, are holy, and that every moment we experience is a gift. Rather than focusing on what we don't have, or on the emotions that arise during specific challenges, we should concentrate *each day* on the positive attributes of what we *do* have in our lives, and make conscious choices to celebrate that. We may also focus our gratitude each day on what new experiences and greater expanded awareness we may envision and create for ourselves as we become more of Who We truly Are. Appreciation of *each* day's specialness will enhance our ability to truly participate in the joy of living.

Laarkmaa would say: *Choose* **gratitude and appreciation in each present moment.**

5 ~ Honor thy father and thy mother.

Our true parents are the stars and the earth. The stars and the earth join together in cooperation to create a home for our experience. We are first from the stars, divinely connected to the universal energy of Source. We must honor that connection within ourselves by taking responsibility for our own light energy and cooperating with one another. We are equally part of and connected to Earth. Because we are here on Earth, we must honor our relationship to Nature. Earth is our home at this time; She gives us the vehicle to experience all aspects of duality, and the opportunity to weave them together into a beautiful, harmonic world of cooperation, peace, and unity.

Laarkmaa would say: *Choose* **to honor the Stars and Earth, and cooperate with one another.**

6 ~ Thou shalt not kill.

This guideline supports the honoring of *all* life. It guides us away from killing through aggression, competition, greed, or war. Yet this guideline is not only about murder, or the taking of human life. This guideline is also meant to lead us away from killing for food. There is no such thing as "killing with kindness" or the "humane" taking of life. All life is a gift, and we do not have the right to take the life of *any* other living being. Because we are all connected, every time we take the life of another (human, animal, or any other life form), we are equally harming ourselves and all others, as well as those we kill. When we eat something we have killed, we are ingesting the energy of death, which *never* supports life. We need to recognize our continuous connection with All That Is, and refrain from *all* killing, instead choosing to honor *all* of life.

Laarkmaa would say: *Choose* **life.** *Choose* **a diet and a lifestyle that reject any form of killing and support the highest good for all.**

7 ~ Thou shalt not commit adultery.

Intimacy is a special gift of sharing with one another, and intimacy should only be engaged through making a lasting commitment to one person, supported by unconditional love, respect, honesty, and transparency. In the third dimension, only such a committed relationship can offer the safety needed to share our total essence; any other type of relationship does not. We must also be whole within ourselves in order to share completely with another. We cannot expect to fill a lonely void within us by engaging in casual sexual encounters. Adultery is not just breaking the vows of marriage; it is breaking the vow to oneself to honor our own sacredness. This means we must never *take* from another person in order to fulfill our own needs; we must fill *ourselves* with love *first*, and then offer to share that love with another. This exquisite and perfect form of intimacy can only be experienced within the trust of a wholly (holy) committed relationship. Adultery is not only experienced through our physical actions; it is also experienced through any *thoughts* that separate us from our partner and committed relationship. We are also committing adultery even when we have a desirous thought about another who is outside of our committed relationship. We commit adultery every time we are dishonest with our partners, whether that dishonesty is in thoughts, words, or physical actions. Ultimately, we must be committed to and responsible for all of our choices. Each choice must be made from the heart, for the highest good for all. If it hurts another, it is not a higher vibratory choice.

Laarkmaa would say: *Choose* **to commit to intimacy with appropriate thoughts and behaviors.**

8 ~ Thou shalt not steal.

Abundance is always available for all of us; therefore there is never any need to steal. To promote the material realization of our abundance, we must begin to understand and engage in *proper energetic exchange.* Everything in the universe is comprised of energy, which moves in a universal flow. That flow is freely available to all, yet it is our individual and collective responsibility *to give back* when we receive, thereby continuing the flow. Humanity has become unbalanced, preferring to receive something that is "free" or to take what we want, rather than honoring the divine flow of universal abundance. We have forgotten the joy of giving. Giving back is comprised of a deep understanding that something of equal value must be exchanged in order to share in universal abundance. When we take something without giving an equal exchange, we are, in effect, *stealing*. When we steal from one person, we steal from all. Through the energy of stealing, we betray the trust of everyone. When humanity finally understands and fully lives from this principle of *proper energetic exchange,* poverty, greed, and lack will simply cease to exist.

Laarkmaa would say: *Choose* **to practice giving and receiving through equal, balanced, and proper exchange.**

9 ~ Thou shalt not bear false witness against thy neighbor.

Again we are guided to be responsible for how we "speak" one another into being. We are directed to tell the truth about one another, but when human emotions become entangled with judgmental thoughts, we often make poor choices and say things that are thoughtless, mean, or not entirely true, using heartless and hurtful tones. Rather than judging one another or competing with one another, we need to respect our fundamental differences as important elements of the whole. No one person, community, country, religion, or idea is more important than the unity we all share together, and thinking or speaking through judgment only separates us. Thinking or speaking unkindly about someone lowers the vibrational field of both the speaker and the one being spoken about. It is much easier to be the highest versions of ourselves when others speak about our virtues, rather than focusing upon our faults. We must learn to be kind, honest, and transparent in how we relate with one another.

Laarkmaa would say: *Choose* **to relate with kindness, transparency, and truth.**

10 ~ Thou shalt not covet what belongs to another.

This idea relates to comparing ourselves to others and judging the differences. Each of us has unique and differing gifts and talents that are ours alone; those gifts cannot and should not be compared to anyone else's, as being greater or lesser attributes and contributions. It is useless to wish to own what belongs to another, including wishing for bigger houses, newer cars, higher salaries, better-looking spouses, specific abilities, or anything else that superficially makes us feel that we are superior. What materializes in our own lives is *directly* related to who *we* are and the choices that we make. When we become thankful for what is ours, rather than wishing to possess what belongs to another, we experience an internal peace that radiates outwardly as love. True freedom comes when we cease to compare ourselves or others and simply appreciate our differences.

Laarkmaa would say: *Choose* **to appreciate and share all that you are and all that you have.**

The "Noble Eightfold Path to Wisdom"

Guidelines from the Buddhist religion are based upon making choices that are balanced and encourage us to behave ethically and with wisdom, and to grow in our understanding. These principles can also be viewed through Laarkmaa's holistic perspective.

1 ~ Right View

This guideline is related to seeing everything in life accurately. We cannot see the truth if we are seeing through our personal filters or our individual or collective beliefs. We must look beyond the Veil of Illusion to have a correct and balanced view of life.

Laarkmaa would say: Move beyond the Veil of Illusion to see the true reality.

2 ~ Right Intention

This guideline instructs us to take personal responsibility for everything that we think, say, or do. When we are conscious of the choices we make, it helps us to intend the highest outcome for all in any situation. Intention must be part of every conscious choice we make in order to manifest harmony and balance for everyone.

Laarkmaa would say: Be responsible; co-create through responsible intentions.

3 ~ Right Speech

We already know the importance of speaking each other into being. Speech is as important as intention because it is equally necessary for proper manifestation. The power of sound propels our intentions into the world through our speech. Right speech is simply taking responsibility for the words and tones that we use with one another.

Laarkmaa would say: Use tones and words that reflect love to co-create your reality.

4 ~ Right Action

Our actions should be preceded by conscious, responsible, and intentional thoughts. Too often we respond to life in a reactive manner, rather than in a compassionate manner. Our actions contribute to and flavor what we create in our physical world. If we want a world of harmony, then we must always allow our hearts to lead us to make compassionate choices in how we act.

Laarkmaa would say: Choose compassion in all of your actions.

5 ~ Right Livelihood

This principle relates to how we share our gifts and talents. Obviously, we should never engage in activities that are not for the highest good for all, nor should we take from others without giving something in return ourselves. Right livelihood is living every moment through the understanding of proper energetic exchange, and following the Golden Rule: "Do unto others as you would have them do unto you."

Laarkmaa would say: InLak'Ech ("I am another yourself.") Live through remembering that you are connected to one another.

6 ~ Right Effort

Use your will power to direct your thoughts, so that all of your efforts result in actions that are led by your heart. When your energy is naturally expended with a sense of joy, all of your effort becomes play rather than work and benefits everyone.

Laarkmaa would say: Use your will to direct your intentions through your heart, and you will find joy in all of your efforts.

7 ~ Right Mindfulness

Right mindfulness is very simple. When our thoughts are connected to our hearts, we are in balance and in harmony. Disconnected, chaotic thoughts cannot occur when our hearts are involved. The mind cannot lead our choices without the heart's wisdom.

Laarkmaa would say: Connect your hearts and minds, and become whole and balanced human beings.

8 ~ Right Concentration

Concentration requires applying responsibility to every thought we have. Without focusing our thoughts to make decisions for the highest good of all, we can never achieve a balanced and healthy state of unity. We need to concentrate on what is truly important, and that is only love and light.

Laarkmaa would say: You are more powerful than you know. Concentrate on truth, trust, love, compassion, and joy to co-create your reality.

While the preceding "Eightfold Path" and the "Ten Commandments" dictate rules that we should follow to live better lives according to the interpretation of specific religions, we feel it is much more powerful to create our own guidelines through our direct connection to divine Source. We are not separating ourselves from God by doing this; rather we are accepting responsibility for the power of our own *choice* in co-creating reality. Laarkmaa assures us that love is the greatest power in the universe, but reminds us that the greatest power we have as humans is the power of choice.

What we deeply know and trust is that *everything* we experience is created by and affected through the choices we make, beginning with *where* we focus our attention, *what* thoughts we think, and *how* we utilize our feelings. Laarkmaa has guided us chapter by chapter, through all the elements involved in making higher vibratory choices, interweaving chapter by chapter, all aspects of choice, from mental, mathematical, symbolic, physical, and energetic perspectives. They even matched the information they provided to the mathematical energy of the numbered chapter in which it was placed. Their wisdom brings us to the place where we can finally and fully understand how *everything* harmoniously blends together in a healthy whole, and how we can co-create a peaceful world in flow and unity.

We will end this book by briefly reviewing all of the aspects Laarkmaa has presented in each chapter, giving you our perspective on the *choices* we are being offered. Drawing from the wisdom Laarkmaa has so lovingly given humanity, we offer here a somewhat different but *equally powerful* set of guidelines for living our lives from the space of love. Because Laarkmaa continually tells us that we always have choice, we call *these* guidelines for living *The Ten Choices*. We will summarize what Laarkmaa shared in each of the ten chapters, including a choice that connects to each chapter's wisdom.

The Ten Choices

The First Choice: *Choose* love.

In Chapter 1, explaining that everything is energy, Laarkmaa told us that all that is necessary to heal is to remember Who We Are. The number one energetically carries the energy of unity, All That Is, and love. The color pink expresses love and is related to the energy of one and unity.

The Second Choice: *Choose* trust.

In Chapter 2, Laarkmaa explained how we have been experiencing life through a Veil of Illusion that creates a dualistic split of opposites. The energy of two represents duality. Laarkmaa explained how when we begin to cooperate rather than to compete with one another, we can use the opposites of duality more effectively. Through the elimination of our belief systems, we can heal all the splits and reconfigure the pieces into a pattern that includes *all* elements in one harmonic whole. We must set aside our fears and begin to trust in one another and in the goodness of the universe to achieve this new pattern. The color blue infuses us with the energy of trust in order to do this.

The Third Choice: *Choose* to create new perspectives for cooperation rather than competition.

In Chapter 3, Laarkmaa explained the energies of creativity, healing, and growth. The number three mathematically represents the vibration of this trinity. They showed us how we have been misunderstanding and misusing the many gifts of the third dimension, and how we can begin our healing process through changing our perspectives. One of the most fundamental perspectives we must change is our belief that we must compete rather than cooperate. The color green carries energies of healing and creativity to support our growth in this process.

The Fourth Choice: *Choose* to be compassionate.

Laarkmaa gave us a new foundation for building a peaceful world in Chapter 4. Mathematically, four represents the energy of foundation and stability. The color gold imparts the energies of both compassion and grace. When we are compassionate, grace fills us with light so that we may see how to proceed and we may build our foundation with the energies of compassion, trust, joy, and love.

The Fifth Choice: *Choose* transcendence.

Chapter 5 is filled with exercises to promote the changes we need to make. In the third dimension, change is the only constant. Life is filled with change; change carries us towards the multidimensional constant of love. The number five carries the energy of change, and use of the color violet helps us to transform, transmute, and transcend whatever needs changing. When we are resistant to change, holding on to old beliefs or old patterns of behavior, we must realize that we are stuck; yet we can transcend *anything*. When we open to transcendence and transformation, we make higher choices for our own evolution.

The Sixth Choice: *Choose* truth.

All of us want to know our life purpose. Because we want to know that we are making a difference, we often struggle with questions about how we are spending our precious moments on Earth. We know that we came here for a reason, yet sometimes our third-dimensional perspectives limit our understanding of just what that reason is. In Chapter 6, Laarkmaa explained our purpose here on Earth from their Pleiadian perspective. The energy of six is mathematically related to flow, and when we are "in the flow," we are connected to universal love, light, and truth. Laarkmaa has used the color white, which represents the purity of truth, to relate to our ability to flow when we are listening to and in harmony with universal truth. The color white is sometimes called Christ light and is often seen in the auras around enlightened beings who understand the proper flow of energy. We will always know our purpose if we choose to release our own belief systems and open to the flow of universal truth.

The Seventh Choice: *Choose* to illuminate your lives with joy.

In Chapter 7, Laarkmaa offered us the seven components of healing, as seen from their much broader multidimensional perspective. These seven components are energy, movement, water, light, sound, Nature, and liquid time. When we honor these gifts, understand them, and use them together, we gain the ability to heal all imbalances and return to our true state of health. The number seven represents magic and gives us an energetic portal to help us step beyond our third-dimensional limitations. The color yellow expresses joy and illumination. Through the presence of the energies of the color yellow and the number seven, we can eliminate the Veil of Illusion and become illuminated by the truth. That illumination fills us with joy of remembering Who We Are and what we are doing here on Earth. If we simply follow our hearts, we will find joy.

The Eighth Choice: *Choose* to connect.

Laarkmaa gave us a rainbow of healing essences in Chapter 8, using the energy of eight to illustrate the infinity of love and our connection to *all*. Laarkmaa lovingly wove together an intrinsic fabric of color energies that we can wear to heal ourselves. This magical fabric is made of love, trust, creativity, compassion, transformation, truth, joy, and connection. The color silver represents the energy of connection and helps us to join all of the elements we need together in order to heal our planet and ourselves.

The Ninth Choice: *Choose* harmony.

Chapter 9 is about harmony. The number nine is mathematically aligned with the energy of harmony. Laarkmaa gave us some new principles and explained more clearly some very old principles about Who We Are and how we must engage with one another. Honesty, or transparency, is essential for our healing, for without complete and total honesty (with ourselves first and then with others), we can never achieve the safety we need to be able to completely trust and to fully love. Additionally, rebalancing ourselves by accepting that *each* of us carries both the Divine Feminine and the Divine Masculine equally within us, leads us even more into a state of harmony. We are androgynous beings full of love and light, here on a planet that needs the expression of *all* of our combined energy to bring harmony to the world. When each of us joins all aspects of ourselves into a complete androgynous whole, and we live in transparency with one another, we can finally achieve harmony and peace on Earth. In this state, we can create a *real* community. Laarkmaa says the energy of nine represents harmony and contains a rainbow of all colors beautifully interwoven together. We can use this rainbow of harmonious energies to guide our choices in each present moment.

> **The Tenth Choice:** *Choose* **to be aware, to be responsible, and to make choices from the heart in** *every* **present moment. We need to achieve this to complete our purpose: to heal humanity by remembering Who We Are.**

This, the tenth chapter, is about manifestation. Laarkmaa has not given us a specific color to represent manifestation, for it is up to us how we choose to apply the appropriate color energies involved with each co-creation. Mathematically, the energy of ten represents manifestation. We manifest our world through each choice we make, individually and together. Each choice carries an energy that flows out into the world, creating new combinations of energies that offer more and more possibilities, in a constant stream of change that brings us closer and closer to the energy of Home. When we use our human power of choice moment by moment to meld all possibilities into a reality that is for the highest good of all, we will awaken and remember. Thank you for being on this journey with us.

Our Choices for Evolution

The First Choice: *Choose* love.

The Second Choice: *Choose* trust.

The Third Choice: Choose to create new perspectives for cooperation rather than competition.

The Fourth Choice: *Choose* to be compassionate.

The Fifth Choice: *Choose* transcendence.

The Sixth Choice: *Choose* truth.

The Seventh Choice: *Choose* to illuminate our lives with joy.

The Eighth Choice: *Choose* to connect.

The Ninth Choice: *Choose* harmony.

The Tenth Choice: *Choose* to be aware, to be responsible, and to make choices from the heart in *every* present moment.

A Final Note From Laarkmaa

We appreciate Cullen and Pia's insights in writing this, the tenth chapter. There are three more chapters to write in the book of Remembering:

Chapter 11 on Illumination,

Chapter 12 on Understanding, and

Chapter 13 on Completion, or Full Ascension into Rainbow form of a completely healed humanity.

We cannot write these chapters, because *you* have the power of choice, and through that power, *you* will determine how these chapters of humanity's evolution are written. However, it is important to note that there *are three* remaining chapters to be written. Please remember that the energy of three represents creativity, and it is through your use of the power of choice that you can create a healthy and whole new reality. If you choose, you can create the foundation we have suggested, using all of the elements we have explored together in this work that blends our written words with our loving and supportive vibrational energy. We support you with our *love*. We have great *trust* that you will now make creative choices from your hearts. We have great *compassion* for the challenges that you are transcending. And we experience great *joy* in helping you. It is now up to you, Dear Ones, to finish the book of your own evolution.

We love you. Good Always!
LAARKMAA

Afterword: Bad Training

Now that you have been able to read and absorb Laark-maa's perspective on how we can heal ourselves, I would like to offer my perspective. We need to raise our consciousness in order to fulfill the many opportunities we have been given. I describe consciousness as people's awareness of the world around them and what effect their actions have on others. We simply need to be more aware of how everything we do affects everyone and everything.

We all suffer from what I've been calling for many years "Bad Training," and we have received it from a *myriad* of different sources. Bad Training can come from parents or grandparents, and generationally through our so-called ancestral lineage; it can come from our educational experiences; it can come from the societies and cultures in which we live. And let's not forget religion, which has done *so* much damage to so many of us. Even under the guise of love, we *still* receive Bad Training. We have collected so many belief systems and rules about how we are to think and behave that we are sometimes unaware of *exactly* what is guiding our thoughts and our actions. It is our job to finally step away from all of that Bad Training, no matter *where* it came from.

Most of our Bad Training stems from listening to others tell us who we are, rather than simply listening to our own hearts, realizing that we truly do know Who We really Are. It is very important to listen to what Laarkmaa has said about how we as humans "speak" each other into being. We have listened to so many who have told us that we must do this or we must do that, often blindly taking their advice because we thought we had no other choice, or because we thought they knew more than we did. Often we choose to believe them simply because we love them or because we *think* they must love us. We never expect them to steer us in the wrong direction. We have been trained to believe that what an elder, a parent, a friend, a colleague, or a religious leader tells us must be the truth. Almost always we *believe* what they say without relying on our own intuition (First Sense) to show us the truth of Who We Are.

Bad Training can easily develop into hardened beliefs about ourselves that are simply not true. I see belief systems as a package of defenses that we collect to keep ourselves safe. It is easy to speak here about childhood coping mechanisms that we developed to protect ourselves because we knew that what we were being told as children did not match what we knew and remembered about the *true* reality. The coping mechanisms we develop provide us with a *false* sense of safety. As adults, we often don't know or haven't come to the understanding that the mechanisms we used to make ourselves feel safe as children simply won't work as we move into adulthood.

We can also be part of the chain of continuing Bad Training without even realizing it. This is where judgment comes into play. Continuing to *believe* what we have been taught and to *judge* those who do not agree with us only perpetuates the problem. It is of utmost importance not to participate in the Bad Training of others, which means we have to be extremely careful in what we think, what we say, and how we say it, about all others with whom we come into contact.

After watching humanity for so many years, I have observed many patterns that create Bad Training. The point I want to make is that Bad Training is all about how others have tried to mold us into what they *want* us to be. They project onto *us* what they want *themselves* to be because *they* have listened to Bad Training and have not achieved realization of Who They really Are. Through Bad Training, people try to make us be like them, believing that if we are all alike, we will finally be safe. If we don't develop into what they want, they try even harder to change us through applying more rules, more restrictions, and more controls. They attempt to force us to become what they want *us* to be simply because they cannot reach what they want within *themselves.*

Because we have all listened to so much Bad Training, rather than listening to the guidance of our hearts, we have forgotten how to love ourselves. We often project our fears, our beliefs, and our needs onto others because we cannot find or accept the love that naturally exists within us. This lack of ability to love ourselves is a direct reflection of all the Bad Training we have received. We need to be careful about how we speak others into reality through using judgment in order to be *absolutely sure* that *we* do not take part in perpetuating the syndrome of Bad Training.

It is now *essential* to finally and completely break the patterns and cycles of Bad Training. It is time to step away from all of the faulty belief systems about ourselves that have colored and molded us into something other than Who We truly Are.

Cullen Baird Smith

Afterthought: How to Choose More Consciously

If we wish to make conscious choices, we must begin by turning our focus away from others' behavior and towards our own. This requires a change of strategy in our interactions. We must reprogram ourselves to *stop* reacting to others and our environment and instead begin to choose conscious actions, *regardless* of what others are saying or doing. These conscious actions can be as simple as walking away or non-engagement in conflict, learning neither to defend ourselves nor attack others, or quieting ourselves to the degree that we are able to actually listen to the truth in our own hearts. As I (Cullen) always say, "You cannot be in a state of compassion if you are in a state of reaction. And you cannot be in a state of reaction if you are in a state of compassion." A decision to hold our own peace and not to react to others enhances our ability to make every choice from a place of compassion, both for ourselves and for others. As we turn our focus away from the behavior of others and towards our own behavior, we can begin to ask ourselves honest questions about how we are engaging in life. Here are a few questions we find helpful in examining ourselves:

◎ How am I greeting the world with my face (my expressions) and my speech?

◎ Am I expressing negative energy in my thoughts, tones, or speech?

◎ Do I remember that every thought I place in my own water (within my own being) either enhances or pollutes the water of all others and the planet?

◎ Are my tones and words filled with kindness, compassion, and love?

◎ Am I actively taking responsibility for what is mine to change?

◎ Am I inappropriately taking responsibility for what is *not* mine?

◎ Am I looking for goodness, rather than flaws?

◎ How am I being unconscious in my habitual behaviors?

◎ How am I being thoughtless or insensitive to others?

◎ Are the differences I notice attached to emotions and beliefs?

◎ Am I searching for truth or clinging to my own beliefs?

◎ What do I believe that keeps me stuck?

◎ How are my perceptions incorrect?

◎ Do I spend enough time connecting in Nature?

◎ Am I being quiet enough to *really* listen?

The questions above refer to choices in our actions as governed by our thoughts; they are examples of how to apply *The Ten Choices* in our daily activities and interactions. As we ask ourselves these questions, it becomes easier and easier to make better choices consciously. As we consider the above questions and suggestions, we find Laarkmaa's wise counsel interwoven through each word. *The Ten Choices*, compiled from Laarkmaa's comprehensive wisdom, will certainly guide us into our own healing and the remembrance of Who We Are.

Pia Smith Orleane & Cullen Baird Smith

What is a Personal Synchronization?

Cullen and Pia provide an opportunity for you to have a private conversation with their Pleiadian friends. Laarkmaa's personal synchronizations are all about *you* and your own evolution. These wonderful star beings synchronize their energy with yours to support you in your own growth as you ask questions and receive their perspectives. You direct the session. (Laarkmaa always empowers people to resolve their own issues, but they also give clear guidance on blocks in energy and blocks in one's own perspective.) Each session is different, as each individual is different, but they generally include helping you to find answers to questions that are important to you, and dissolving or clearing energetic blocks that exist within your system so that you may move forward with more clarity, ease, and power within your own life. We record each session for you to hear and absorb their wisdom again later.

Comments from some of the people around the world who have received Personal Synchronizations are listed below. You will find a more comprehensive list of comments on our website. The number of Personal Synchronizations available is *limited*. To request the possibility for a Personal Synchronization with Laarkmaa, please follow the instructions listed at www.laarkmaa.com.

REMEMBERING WHO WE ARE

WORLDWIDE ENDORSEMENTS

ENGLAND:
"My time spent with Laarkmaa was nothing less than extraordinary!" CS

THE NETHERLANDS:
"A life-changing experience! They helped me step further into my True Self." CB

FRANCE:
"I had the feeling of being cradled in loving arms, and their presence has stayed with me ever since." Lesley

SWEDEN:
"The 'time' that I was given with Laarkmaa gave me a quantum leap in peace as well as clear signposts on how to see myself and others." Nick

BELGIUM:
"It was tremendously beautiful. I still feel the energy working through my body, and new insights are rising, too!" Rachel

SINGAPORE:
"I am ever grateful to Laarkmaa. Their loving energy and their encouragement to find creative solutions empowers me more than ever." O

TURKEY:
"Absolutely incredible! I was able to ask specific questions, receive healing energy, and hear Laarkmaa's perspective on things I am trying to shift in my life." Marla

NEW JERSEY, USA:
"I am forever changed for the better because of Laarkmaa." John

ILLINOIS, USA:

"In just 24 hours since the session with Laarkmaa, I know
I am a different person. Focused, calm, and more trusting
than ever." Sophia

ONTARIO, CANADA:

"Laarkmaa gently shared so much wisdom to help me on my
personal journey." Brian

CALIFORNIA, USA

"In an era of increasing confusion, Laarkmaa gives precise
examples of how to orient ourselves toward a new
consciousness through love and helps us release the feelings
of fear, moving forward with truth and awareness." EC

NEW ZEALAND:

"One hour with Laarkmaa was more valuable than years of
therapy." RS

SWEDEN:

"Sometimes before I asked, Laarkmaa answered questions
I didn't even know I had. They understood my need of
guidance, which was amazing!" Diana

ARIZONA, USA:

"A synchronization with Laarkmaa is an invitation to
remove whatever is blocking us, a life-changing experience."
Janeen

WASHINGTON, USA:

"It touched us profoundly. We are already feeling
multi-levels of change within us." Resha & Stanley

CALIFORNIA, USA:

"I love Laarkmaa. I will definitely schedule another session
and highly recommend sessions for others." Ross

MICHIGAN, USA:

"Connecting to Laarkmaa on a one-on-one basis is very freeing because there is no judgment, ever, only unconditional love and really, really insightful information." Scott

OREGON, USA:

"They helped me remove some major blocks in my heart, showing me how to make better decisions about my life." Lora

TEXAS, USA:

"Synchronizing with Laarkmaa was truly a life-changing event for me, as I was able to be brought to a place of greater peace and harmony." Debbie

BRITISH COLUMBIA, CANADA:

"My synchronization with Laarkmaa was wonderful! I would highly recommend a Personal Synchronization." Pat

CALIFORNIA, USA:

"It turned on a light for me. Insights that I received about my father have changed the way I now think of him. Looking forward to future conversations!" RW

OREGON, USA:

"Experiencing a personal synchronization with Laarkmaa is remembering what you have always known." Barakah

ABOUT THE AUTHORS

LAARKMAA is a loving group of Pleiadians who are dedicated to the evolution of humanity. They have chosen Pia Orleane and Cullen Smith to be their Ambassadors on Earth. Through their love, wisdom, and higher perspective, Laarkmaa offers messages of peace, hope, and harmony, guiding us all towards a greater understanding of love, light, and unity.

PIA SMITH ORLEANE has accessed parallel realms of Love and Light, including interstellar beings, fairies, and angels, since she was a small child. Pia (formerly known as "Rebecca") experienced a mysterious energetic illness that caused her to step more fully into Who She Is and change her name to Pia, which means "Sacred." Love is the heart and essence of Pia's life. Pia Smith Orleane holds a Ph.D. in the Psychology of Consciousness. She joins Cullen Baird Smith in the joyous life work and complete partnership of bringing Laarkmaa's love and wisdom to the world for the evolution of humanity.

Pia's other works include *Conversations With Laarkmaa, A Pleiadian View of the New Reality*, co-authored with Cullen Baird Smith; COVR Award Winning Visionary Fiction *Southern Piercings*; and the definitive book on cycles of Nature, *The Return of the Feminine.*

CULLEN BAIRD SMITH is a Visionary, a Sensitive, and an Interstellar Communicator. Cullen has participated with non-ordinary states of reality with interstellar beings and Pan's kingdom since early childhood. Cullen began using energy to support the healing of others when he was four years old. Preceding the magical Findhorn Gardens in Scotland by a decade, he co-created a "Findhorn Garden" in his own backyard at the age of seven.

Cullen has focused his life on assisting *all* in the evolutionary movement towards unity. He joins Pia Smith Orleane in the joy of bringing forth Laarkmaa, a Pleiadian group dedicated to raising human consciousness. Together, Cullen and Pia have dedicated their lives to bringing Laarkmaa's voice to the world. Cullen is co-author of Laarkmaa's earlier work *Conversations With Laarkmaa, A Pleiadian View of the New Reality.*

To learn more about Laarkmaa, Pia, Cullen, and Laarkmaa's future Center of Love and Light, or to schedule a personal session with Laarkmaa, please visit: www.laarkmaa.com